Structural Equation Modelling (SEM) Made Easy
for Business and Social Science Research Using SPSS and AMOS

SHEENA LOVIA BOATENG

Structural Equation Modelling (SEM) Made Easy for Business and Social Science Research Using SPSS and AMOS

All rights reserved. No part of this *publication* may be reproduced, distributed, or transmitted in any form or by any means, including photocopying, recording, or other electronic or mechanical methods, without the prior written permission of the publisher, except in the case of *brief quotations* embodied in critical reviews and certain other noncommercial uses permitted by copyright law. For permission requests, write to the publisher at the address below.

Author:

SHEENA LOVIA **BOATENG**

Email: lovia@pearlrichards.org

Copyright © 2018 Sheena Lovia Boateng

Kindle Direct Publishing
Printed by Kindle Direct Publishing, An Amazon.com Company
Seattle, Washington

ISBN: 9781730806704
Independently Published

To My Husband and Daughter

You Mean The World To Me

Preface

You are welcome to Structural Equation Modelling (SEM) Made Easy for Business and Social Science Research Using SPSS and Amos. This book seeks to provide a simple practical guide to conducting quantitative data analysis. First, it presents an overview of quantitative research, by explaining different types of variables and the formulation and testing of hypotheses. Second, it presents the rubrics for designing quantitative questionnaires, explains sampling and illustrates how to determine sample size. Third, the book also explains descriptive statistics and how to conduct and present descriptive statistics in a research write-up. Fourth, it provides a step by step process to carry out exploratory factor analysis and procedures for interpreting related outputs from the statistical software package, SPSS. Fifth, it teaches how to establish reliability and validity in quantitative research.

Finally, the book explains the basics of Structural Equation Modelling (SEM) and demonstrates the two-step approach to SEM analysis, the foundational concepts of measurement models, structural models, Confirmatory Factor Analysis (CFA) and Path Analysis (PA). It also teaches how to run SEM analysis using Amos, and how to interpret the resulting output.

This book is essential for anyone involved in business and social science research. Its purpose is not to create a 'one best format', but to offer a practical guide in analyzing quantitative data and presenting such analysis in research papers, long essays, theses and dissertations.

Table of Contents

CHAPTER 1 11

BASICS OF QUANTITATIVE RESEARCH 11

OBJECTIVES 11
What is Quantitative Research? 12
Selecting a Quantitative Data Analysis Technique 14
Types of Variables 16
Categorical and Continuous Variables 16
Dependent, Independent and Control Variables 18
Mediating and Moderating Variables 19
Illustration 1 – Types of Variables 21
Hypothesis Formulation 22
What are Hypotheses? 22
Types of Hypotheses 23
Hypothesizing Relationships between Variables 23
Hypothesis Testing 25
Illustration 2 – Hypotheses Formulation and Testing using the p-value method 26
Chapter Summary 28
Chapter Review 29

CHAPTER 2 33

QUESTIONNAIRE DESIGN 33

OBJECTIVES 33
Why Design a Questionnaire? 34
How to Design a Good Questionnaire 35
Questionnaire Layout 42
Illustration 3 - Sample Questionnaire 44
Chapter Summary 51
Chapter Review 52

CHAPTER 3

SAMPLING

OBJECTIVES

Selecting a Sample
- Probability or Representative Sampling
- Non-probability Sampling

Determining Appropriate Sample Size
- Taro Yamane's Formula for Sample Size
- Illustration 4
- Cochran's Sample Size Formula
- Illustration 5

Chapter Summary
Chapter Review

CHAPTER 4

DESCRIPTIVE STATISTICS

OBJECTIVES

What are Descriptive Statistics?
- Frequency Distribution
- Measures of Central Tendency
- Measures of Dispersion

Practical Demonstration
- Procedure in SPSS

Chapter Review
- Illustration 6 – Profile of Respondents

Chapter Summary

CHAPTER 5

EXPLORATORY FACTOR ANALYSIS (EFA)

OBJECTIVES

What is Exploratory Factor Analysis (EFA)?
The 5-Step Exploratory Factor Analysis Protocol
- Data Suitability

Factor Extraction *85*
Factor Rotation *87*
Factor Interpretation and Labeling *88*
Factor Transformation *88*
PRACTICAL DEMONSTRATION OF EXPLORATORY FACTOR ANALYSIS (EFA) – PCA 89
Procedure in SPSS *89*
Factor Transformation *100*
Analyzing Exploratory Factor Analysis (EFA) Output *102*
EXPLORATORY FACTOR ANALYSIS (EFA) FOR SEM 103
Procedure in SPSS *103*
CHAPTER SUMMARY 112
CHAPTER REVIEW 113

CHAPTER 6 115

RELIABILITY AND VALIDITY 115

OBJECTIVES 115
WHY RELIABILITY AND VALIDITY? 116
ASSESSING RELIABILITY 117
Practical Demonstration of Reliability Tests *119*
Analyzing the Output *124*
ASSESSING VALIDITY 133
CHAPTER SUMMARY 134
CHAPTER REVIEW 135

CHAPTER 7 137

STRUCTURAL EQUATION MODELLING (SEM) – THE BASICS 137

OBJECTIVES 137
WHAT IS STRUCTURAL EQUATION MODELLING (SEM)? 138
SEM Nomenclature *139*
SEM Notation *140*
PERFORMING SEM ANALYSIS 141
Model Specification *141*
Model Identification *142*
Model Estimation *142*

Model Testing *143*
Model Modification *146*
CHAPTER SUMMARY 147

CHAPTER 8 149

STRUCTURAL EQUATION MODELLING (SEM) - THE TWO-STAGE APPROACH 149

OBJECTIVES 149
WHY THE TWO-STAGE APPROACH? 150
Stage 1 - Measurement Stage *150*
Stage 2 - Structural Stage *151*
PRACTICAL DEMONSTRATION OF THE TWO-STAGE APPROACH TO SEM 153
Procedure for Stage 1 - Measurement Stage using Amos *154*
ANALYZING CONFIRMATORY FACTOR ANALYSIS (CFA) OUTPUT 167
Procedure for Stage 2 - Structural Stage using Amos *168*
Nested Models *173*
CHAPTER SUMMARY 176

CHAPTER 9 179

PRACTICAL DEMONSTRATION OF STRUCTURAL EQUATION MODELLING (SEM) IN A THESIS FORMAT 179

OBJECTIVES 179
PRELIMINARY DATA PREPARATION 180
SAMPLE CHARACTERISTICS 180
DESCRIPTIVE STATISTICS 183
EXPLORATORY FACTOR ANALYSIS (EFA) 186
Rotation and Reliability of the EFA *187*
ASSESSMENT OF COMMON METHOD VARIANCE (CMV) 190
POST-STUDY FRAMEWORK 191
ANALYSIS AND RESULTS OF STRUCTURAL EQUATION MODELLING 191
Stage 1 - Measurement Phase *194*
Validity and Reliability of Final Measurement Model *199*
Stage 2 - Structural Model *201*
Model Comparison *204*
CHAPTER SUMMARY 207

REFERENCES 208
INDEX 212

AUTHOR PROFILE **213**

List of Figures and Tables

FIGURE 1 - SAMPLE CONCEPTUAL FRAMEWORK 21
FIGURE 2 - EFFECTS OF ENGAGEMENT, INTERACTIVITY, ADVOCACY AND PERSONALIZATION ON AFFECTIVE CUSTOMER COMMITMENT, THE MEDIATING ROLE OF TRUST 27
FIGURE 3 - AGE OF RESPONDENTS 78
FIGURE 4 - EFA PROTOCOL 83
FIGURE 5 - SEM NOTATION IN AMOS 140
FIGURE 6 - SEM BUILDING BLOCKS 141
FIGURE 7 - CUT-OFF CRITERIA FOR FIT INDICES[62] 144

FIGURE 9.1 POST-STUDY FRAMEWORK 193
FIGURE 9.2 FINAL CFA MEASUREMENT MODEL 198
FIGURE 9.3 HYPOTHESISED STRUCTURAL MODEL 202
FIGURE 9.4 FINAL STRUCTURAL MODEL 206

TABLE 1 - TABLE OF ITEMS AND THEIR MEASURES[13] 37
TABLE 2 - PROFILE OF RESPONDENTS 78
TABLE 3 - CONSTRUCT MEASURES AND DESCRIPTIVE STATISTICS 79
TABLE 4 - LOADINGS TABLE[31] 132
TABLE 5 - CORRELATION MATRIX WITH AVEs[31] 134
TABLE 6 - ALTERNATIVE MODEL COMPARISON[13] 175

TABLE 9.1 PROFILE OF RESPONDENTS 181
TABLE 9.2 CONSTRUCT MEASURES AND DESCRIPTIVE STATISTICS 183
TABLE 9.3 KMO AND BARTLETT'S TEST 186
TABLE 9.4 ROTATED FACTOR MATRIX AND INTERNAL CONSISTENCIES 188
TABLE 9.5 FIT INDICES FOR MEASUREMENT MODEL 194
TABLE 9.6 MEASUREMENT MODEL ITEMS AND THEIR DESCRIPTION 195
TABLE 9.7 CFA RESULTS FOR FINAL MEASUREMENT MODEL 199
TABLE 9.8 CORRELATION MATRIX WITH AVEs 200
TABLE 9.9 HYPOTHESES TEST RESULTS 202
TABLE 9.10 RESULTS OF ALTERNATIVE MODEL COMPARISONS 205

Chapter 1

Basics of Quantitative Research

OBJECTIVES

This chapter seeks to introduce readers to the building blocks of quantitative research and data analysis. At the end of this chapter, it is expected that readers will know the variety of data analysis software that exist, the types of data and what goes into selecting a multivariate data analysis technique for a given research. They will also understand what goes into hypothesis formulation and testing.

What is Quantitative Research?

Quantitative research is a systematic approach to the investigation of a concept or phenomenon, which involves the direct collection of numerical data and/or transformation of observations by the researcher into numerical data for computational purposes. Quantitative research is usually applied in finding evidence to substantiate assertions made by the researcher during hypotheses formulation in the early stages of the research process. The application of rational and critical thinking is required during quantitative research, since researchers must critically analyze and objectively interpret findings from the data by comparing it to other findings within the framework of the research, as well as existing literature on the subject matter. As such, selecting the appropriate data analysis technique for a given research is important; since that is what will enable the researcher to successfully address the quantifiable aims and objectives of their study. Various statistical software and programs exist that facilitate the analysis of quantitative data; including **Microsoft Excel**, **Mplus**, **Minitab**, **R**, **Stata**, **SPSS**, **SAS**, **PLS** and **Amos**, with SPSS being the most popular, especially at the undergraduate level. This software enables the researcher to collate the data collected, prepare and check it. It also provides statistics to enable researchers to generate the most appropriate tables, diagrams and indicators to describe their data and examine relationships and trends in them. The statistical techniques that are utilized can be classified into two main groups, **Descriptive statistics** and **Inferential statistics**. These are best explained in terms of the population and sample used for the study, as we will observe in the ensuing sections.

Population refers to a category or collection of people, objects or items of interest that can be either widely or narrowly defined. For instance, a population can be defined widely as *'all bank customers in Ghana'* or narrowly as *'all PRF Bank retail banking customers in the Greater Accra Region'*. On the other hand, **sample** refers to a portion of the entire population, which if properly taken can be representative of the entire population. Having this understanding, we will now define Descriptive and Inferential statistics.

♣ **Descriptive statistics** are used to describe the basic features of data collected. They are statistics gleaned from data gathered on a given group to describe or reach conclusions about that same group. They provide simple summaries about the research sample and the variables measured in the data set including the range of values, their average, and the most recurring categories. They also use tabular, graphical, and numerical methods to summarize data.

♣ **Inferential statistics** on the other hand, are used to make comparisons, test effects, test causal relationships and draw conclusions from the data. Knowledge gained from inferential statistics allows investigators to make inferences and generalize beyond their study sample to the population from which the sample was drawn. With inferential statistics, you are trying to reach conclusions that extend beyond the immediate data alone.

Statistical methods found under these two groups of statistics include frequencies, regressions, analyses of variance, structural equation modeling among others. A number of these will be discussed in more detail in the ensuing chapters. But before then it is of prime importance to know the right analysis technique to select in order to effectively address the objectives of a given research; as we will observe in the next section.

For the purposes of illustration, the **SPSS** and **Amos** software will be used in demonstrating the various quantitative data analysis techniques that are described and explained throughout this book.

Selecting a Quantitative Data Analysis Technique

There exist several well-developed quantitative data analysis methods and techniques, which are available for the conceptual and statistical analysis of the various forms of data that can be gathered. But, it behooves the researcher to know the different methods that are available to them, taking into consideration their individual strengths in data analysis and the resources available to them. Also, they must have a good understanding of the various differences between the techniques, as well as the associated benefits and limitations of each of them. Having this insight enables the researcher to design an appropriate survey instrument and select the right sample to administer the survey to, in order to obtain data that is relevant to their chosen analysis technique. There are several steps involved in selecting an appropriate data analysis technique as highlighted below. In order to select the appropriate statistical analysis technique, the researcher must:

1. **Clarify what they want to find out, and the research question(s) that they seek to answer**

   The first step in deciding on the correct analysis technique to use is to outline the research question for the study. What is the nature of the research question? Is it a *relational* question, one that seeks information on the relationship between certain variables? Or a *causal* question, one that seeks information about the effect of one variable on another? Or a question of *grouping*, one that seeks to determine the likelihood of a respondent belonging to a particular group based on certain variables? Or even the strength and nature of a connection between two variables? Having a clear understanding of the research question and what it entails, will lead the researcher to choose the correct technique that will help them meet those requirements.

2. **Define the level of measurement for each variable to be included in the analysis**

   The term variable refers to a specific concept about which information is collected in a study. It can be considered as either dependent or independent among others (see section on Types of variables). The researcher needs to determine the level of measurement of each of these variables by outlining which ones will be classified as either categorical data or continuous data; which will be discussed into further detail in the next section. By identifying this the researcher can choose the right statistical technique for their study, since the various techniques each have benefits and limitations in considering different types of variables, at different levels of measurement, be it categorical or continuous.

3. **Select the right statistical technique to enable them to answer their research question(s)**

   There are varied forms of statistical analysis, but here the research question is of prime importance, since the ultimate aim of the study is to answer the research question. Hence, one needs to be specific in stating their research question. The statistical approach to the study must be planned at the start of the project, before any data is collected. This will enable the researcher to plan the manner in which data collection will proceed and enable them to collect only data that is relevant. If the research question is about group differences, the technique needs to be able to compare groups. Also, the researcher must consider the level of measurement of the different variables in their framework (see section on Types of variables). For instance, research question from a given research design will use different statistical methods if the dependent variable is measured as a categorical variable than if it's measured as a continuous variable (see section on Types of variables).

4. Determine the appropriate sample size

The determination of sample size is a common task for several researchers. But, the selection of an inappropriate, inadequate, or excessive sample size has the ability to influence the quality and accuracy of a given research. Therefore, perhaps the most frequently asked question is 'What sample size do I need?' The answer to this question is dependent on a number of criteria, particularly the purpose of the study and the overall size of the population. However, in addition to these other approaches to determining the appropriate sample size, one can use the typical sample sizes which have been used in studies similar to the one that they are conducting. Alternatively, one can use simplified sample size formulae suggested by authors such as Yamane[26] to determine the appropriate sample size. This will be discussed in further detail in subsequent sections.

TYPES OF VARIABLES

Quantitative data is gathered in the form of variables through a survey instrument. A variable as used in this instance refers to a measurable characteristic that has a quantity or quality that varies. These variables are identified based on their unique individual characteristics, which are determined by a number of factors, including the issues and concepts that the researcher intends to study and how these variables are linked to each other in the research framework; as seen in the upcoming sections. These to a large extent determine the forms of statistical analysis that can be run on a given data set.

Categorical and Continuous Variables

Generally, regardless of the role of a given variable in a framework, all constructs in a given quantitative data set usually represent either measurements on some continuous scale or information about some categorical characteristics. Therefore, primarily data can be labeled as either **Categorical** or **Continuous**, with most quantitative data sets containing both categorical and continuous variables.

Categorical Variables

This is data that can be grouped into specific categories. Labels or names are used to identify the attributes or categories of these variables, for instance Gender is either Male or Female, these are the two main categories of gender. Categorical variables use either the **nominal** or **ordinal** scale of measurement. The nominal scale is said to be in use when the data has labels or names used to identify an attribute of a variable and can be either numeric or non-numeric. For example, suppose you are testing three marketing tactics on customers. You call these tactics, Tactics 1, 2, and 3, respectively. These tactics have numerical values, but the numbers do not have any ordering significance. That is, Tactic 1 is not necessarily better than Tactic 3. These numbers serve simply as names for the values of the variable and cannot be numerically compared.

Whereas, an ordinal scale is said to be in use if the data exhibits the properties of nominal data and the rank or order of the data is meaningful. It can also be either numeric or non-numeric. For example, let us assume that Time magazine reports the top three billionaires in the world each year. That is, we have Billionaire 1, 2, and 3, where 1 is considered the richest of the three, 2 the second richest, and 3 the third richest. In this instance, we can say 1 is richer than 2 and 3 and 3 is not as rich as 1 and 2. This type of variable has the properties of a nominal scaled variable, but also has the property of order or ranking.

Continuous Variables

Continuous variables represent data that are measured on a continuum or scale. It can have almost any numeric value and can be meaningfully subdivided into finer and finer increments, depending upon the precision of the measurement system. Continuous variables use either the **interval** or **ratio** scale of measurement. The interval scale is said to be in use when the data are measured along a continuum using numerical values. For example, Temperature is measured in degrees Celsius or Fahrenheit along a continuum, such that the difference between 20^0C and 30^0C is the same as 30^0C to 40^0C.

Whereas, a ratio scale is said to be in use when the data demonstrate all the characteristics of an interval scale, but with the added condition that 0 (zero) of the measurement indicates that there is none of that variable. Hence, temperature measured in degrees Celsius or Fahrenheit is not a ratio variable because 0^0C does not mean there is no temperature. Examples of ratio variables include height, mass, distance and much more. The name 'ratio' reflects the fact that you can use the ratio of measurements. So, for example, a distance of 30 meters is twice the distance of 15 meters. In practice data on continuous variables is gathered using Likert type questions in the form of a survey or questionnaire, which will be discussed in greater detail in the section on questionnaire design.

Dependent, Independent and Control Variables

These are the variables typically found in a given research framework designed for a quantitative study. They are classified based on their position within the research framework and the role that they play in relation to other variables in the framework. Hence, a variable in this instance is not only something that we measure, but also something we can manipulate to cause an effect and also control for. This leads to variables in a given framework being either **Dependent**, **Independent** or **Controls**, as subsequently explained.

Dependent Variables

The dependent variable is exactly that, a variable that is dependent on another variable, which is known as an independent variable. Also referred to as the **Outcome variable**, it is the variable that is affected by the changes that take place in the independent variable or the manipulation of it.

Independent Variables

The independent variable, sometimes called the **Predictor variable**, is a variable that is manipulated in order to observe a change in a dependent variable. The manipulation of the independent variable or changes that take place in it affect the dependent variable; and this can be either positive or negative.

Control Variables

Control variables are the variables that are not of primary interest in a data analysis, and therefore constitute an extraneous or third factor. However, they have the ability to influence the model and hence this influence in the model needs to be controlled for or eliminated. Controlling for a variable or potential confounder is intended to isolate the effect of that variable to enable the researcher to test a relationship of interest that is independent of the influence of that control variable and free from any bias arising from variations in this variable. In this regard control variables are not hypothesized for. Demographic variables (categorical variables) such as gender and age, have often been indicated in literature as very good examples of control variables. However, this is not enough reason to include them as controls, their inclusion must be based on the nature of the study and their relative importance to the study.

Mediating and Moderating Variables
Mediating Variables

These are variables that intervene in the relationship between the dependent and independent variable. Generally, it is a variable that explains how certain physical events take on internal psychological significance in a model, such that they speak to how or why certain effects of independent variables on dependent variables occur.[30] It is the variable that once introduced into the direct relationship between the dependent and independent variable either causes the pre-existing direct relationship between the dependent and independent variable to become diminished (partial mediation) or to disappear completely (full mediation). This is explained further:

- ***Full mediation*** - The complete intervention caused by the mediator variable between the dependent and independent variables. This results in the initial independent variable no longer affecting or having an influence on the dependent variable.
- ***Partial mediation*** - The partial intervention caused by the mediator variable between the dependent and independent variables. This results in the initial independent variable and the mediating variable both affecting or having an influence on the dependent variable.

Moderating Variables

These are variables that have the ability to influence the direction and/ or strength of the causal relationship between an independent and a dependent variable. In relatively more familiar analysis of variance (ANOVA) terms, the effect of a moderating variable can be represented as an interaction between a focal independent variable and another variable that stipulates the appropriate conditions for its operation.[30] Generally it specifies when certain effects of a given independent variable on a dependent variable will hold.

Examples of all these varied types of variables are presented in the ensuing section.

Illustration 1 - Types of Variables

The sample framework, shown in Figure 1, provides an illustration of the different types of variables that have been discussed in sections above. The framework presents some factors that are purported to influence a customer's loyalty to their motor insurer. It depicts that a customer's loyalty to their motor insurer is determined by the cost of their premiums and the promptness with which their insurer pays insurance claims when they fall due. However, this relationship is dependent upon the customer's overall satisfaction with the insurer's services and could be strengthened or weakened by their perceptions of the brand image of the insurer. But, there is also the possibility that the level of income of the insurer and their gender could influence their loyalty. Thus, these are controlled for; as seen in Figure 1 below.

FIGURE 1 - SAMPLE CONCEPTUAL FRAMEWORK

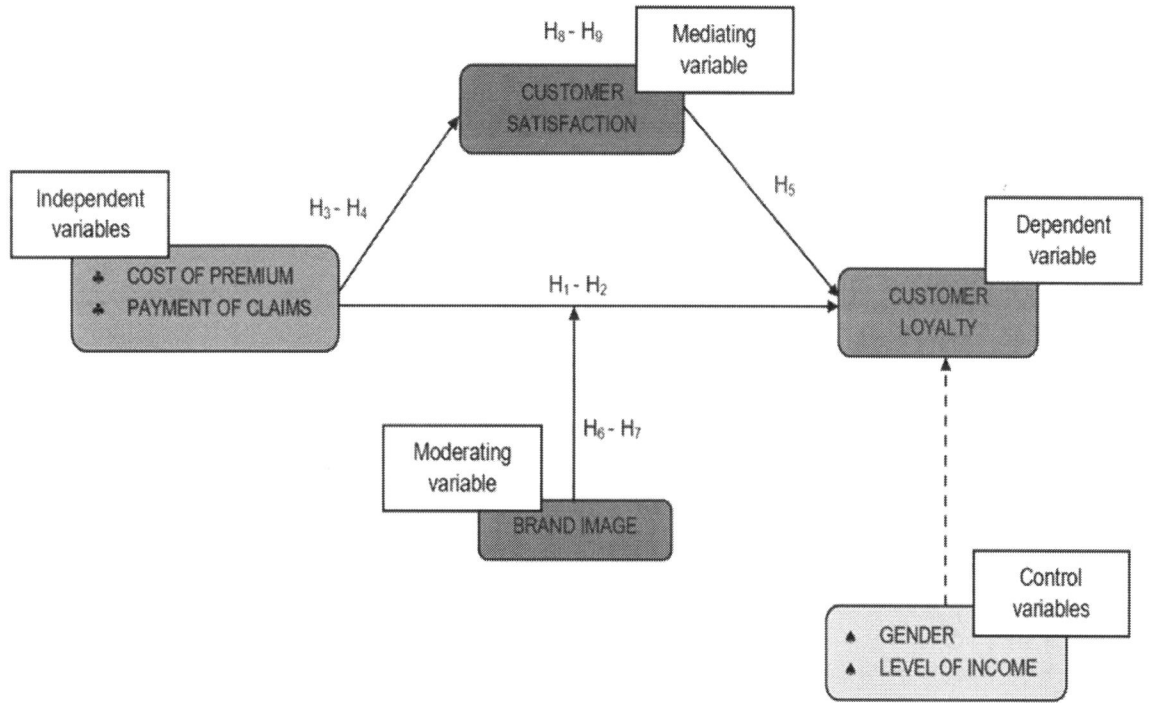

Hypothesis Formulation

A research always begins with an identified problem, for which hypotheses are required to provide clarifications of this research problem.[4] Hypothesis formulation involves the utilization of different variables, as presented above, in putting together specific, testable, and predictable statements that are driven by theory and/or backed by prior evidence.[1] These statements are referred to as hypotheses and constitute the basis of a quantitative research inquiry.

What are Hypotheses?

They are the initial building blocks in quantitative analysis. They are described as an "educated guess," based on prior knowledge and observation. A hypothesis is a statement that is used to explain a phenomenon or predict a relationship between two or more variables. These predictions are only based on limited evidence and used as a starting point for further investigation. As such, their validity is unknown. Therefore, to formulate a good hypothesis there are a number of criteria that a researcher must take cognizance of.[2]

Formulation Criteria

A hypothesis statement must:
1. State an expected relationship between two or more variables.
2. Be testable and falsifiable; meaning that researchers must be able to use valid and reliable data to test it to either prove or disprove it.
3. Be consistent with the existing body of knowledge in the specific area in which the research is being conducted.
4. Be as simple and concise as possible.

Types of Hypotheses

There are two main types of research hypotheses in quantitative data analysis. These are the **null hypothesis** that is represented by H_0 and the **alternative hypothesis,** which is represented by H_a or H_n, where **n** represents the specific number of the hypotheses in question relative to the total number of hypotheses in the study. These are elaborated below.

> *Null hypothesis (H_0)* - A null hypothesis is a hypothesis that indicates that there is no statistically significant relationship between the variables identified by the researcher. This type of hypothesis is the one that a researcher will try to disprove or discredit. It is worthy to note that it is not always mandatory to present the null hypothesis along with the alternative hypothesis in a given research manuscript. This however is largely dependent on the context.

> *Alternative hypothesis (H_a or H_n)* - An alternative hypothesis is a hypothesis that indicates that there is a statistically significant relationship between the variables identified by the researcher. This hypothesis is the one that a researcher seeks to prove and is usually presented as the inverse form of the null hypothesis.[3] The alternative hypothesis is the one usually presented in research manuscripts to indicate the relationships between the variables to be studied.

Hypothesizing Relationships between Variables

As identified in previous sections, different variables play diverse roles and have specific relationships with other variables in a given study, such as dependent, independent or moderating variables. Thus, research hypotheses must be formulated such that the role of the variable being hypothesized for in the study, as well as its relationship to other variables in the study, is made apparent. There are several ways by which hypotheses can be formulated to depict the relationships between variables in a given framework. Examples of these are delineated below, using some of the variables previously presented in Figure 1:

Example 1 - Direct relationships

Cost of premiums have a positive significant effect on customer loyalty.

OR

There is a significant relationship between cost of premiums and customer loyalty.

Example 2 – Mediating relationships

Customer satisfaction mediates the relationship between cost of premiums and customer loyalty.

OR

The significant relationship between cost of premiums and customer loyalty is mediated by customer satisfaction.

Example 3 – Moderating relationships

Brand image moderates the relationship between cost of premiums and customer loyalty.

OR

The significant effect of cost of premiums on customer loyalty is enhanced by brand image.

Hypothesis Testing

To test hypotheses, researchers must utilize the p-value method, the steps for which are presented as follows.[5] The researcher must:

Step 1: State the hypothesis that is to be tested (the alternative hypothesis); and then form a statement for the null hypothesis. This is demonstrated in the hypothesis formulation section.

Step 2: Choose which significance level that they would like to use. A significance level is the threshold value that we measure p-values against; they are typically denoted by the Greek letter alpha 'α'. Here the researcher must consider both Type I and Type II errors. A **Type I error** occurs when we reject a null hypothesis that is actually true. While, a **Type II error** occurs when we fail to reject a null hypothesis that is actually false.[24]

To control for these two types of error, researchers must select the smallest significance level or alpha level. The most common significance levels are **0.05 (5%)**, **0.01 (1%)** and **0.001 (0.1%)**. These are depicted by *****, ****** and ******* respectively. A significance level of 0.05 (5%) means that there is a 5% probability that the test will suffer a Type I error by rejecting a true null hypothesis. This significance level conversely translates to a 95% level of confidence, meaning that over a series of hypothesis tests, 95% will not result in a Type I error.[6] Likewise, a significance level of 0.01 (1%) means that there is a 1% probability that the test will suffer a Type I error by rejecting a true null hypothesis. This significance level conversely translates to a 99% level of confidence, meaning that over a series of hypothesis tests, 99% will not result in a Type I error. Also, a significance level of 0.001 (0.1%) means that there is a 0.1% probability that the test will suffer a Type I error by rejecting a true null hypothesis. This significance level conversely translates to a 99.9% level of confidence, meaning that over a series of hypothesis tests, 99.9% will not result in a Type I error.

Step 3: Evaluate the test statistic and the p-value. Every test statistic has a corresponding p-value. This value is the probability that the observed statistic occurred by chance alone, assuming that the null hypothesis is true. If the p-value is less than or equal to 0.05 (*), we reject the null hypothesis and say that the result is statistically significant, thus the alternative hypothesis stands. But, if the p-value is greater than 0.05 (*), then we fail to reject the null hypothesis and say that the result is not statistically significant.

Step 4: State the results of the hypothesis test in a manner that addresses the researcher's original claim.

Illustration 2 provides a demonstration of how research hypotheses are formulated and tested using the p-value method for a typical quantitative study conducted for publication purposes.

Illustration 2 - Hypotheses Formulation and Testing using the p-value method

Boateng and Narteh[31] researched on the effects of the online relationship marketing practices of engagement, interactivity, advocacy and personalization on affective customer commitment, in addition to the mediating role of trust in the Ghanaian Banking industry. A number of hypotheses were formulated for the study[31], as seen in Figure 2. Among the hypotheses for the study were:

H_1 - Engagement of customers online is positively related to Affective commitment. **(Direct relationship)**

H_2 - Interactivity with customers online is positively related to Affective commitment. **(Direct relationship)**

H_3 - Advocacy by online customers is positively related to Affective commitment. **(Direct relationship)**

H₄ - Personalization with online customers is positively related to Affective commitment. **(Direct relationship)**

H₅ - Collaboration is positively related to Affective commitment. **(Direct relationship)**

H₆₍ₐ₋ₑ₎ - Trust mediates the relationship between the online relationship marketing practices and Affective commitment. **(Mediating relationship)**

Using the p-value method, the study found support for hypotheses **H₃** and **H₅** such that the direct effects of advocacy and collaboration on affective commitment are supported by the significant path coefficients estimated at $p < 0.01$ and $p < 0.05$ respectively. Supporting **H₆ₐ** and **H₆d** trust was found to mediate the relationship between engagement and affective commitment, as well as personalization and affective commitment at $p < 0.05$ respectively. The remaining hypotheses, **H₁, H₂, H₄, H₆b** and **H₆c** were all found to be insignificant at $p > 0.05$.

FIGURE 2 - EFFECTS OF ENGAGEMENT, INTERACTIVITY, ADVOCACY AND PERSONALIZATION ON AFFECTIVE CUSTOMER COMMITMENT, THE MEDIATING ROLE OF TRUST

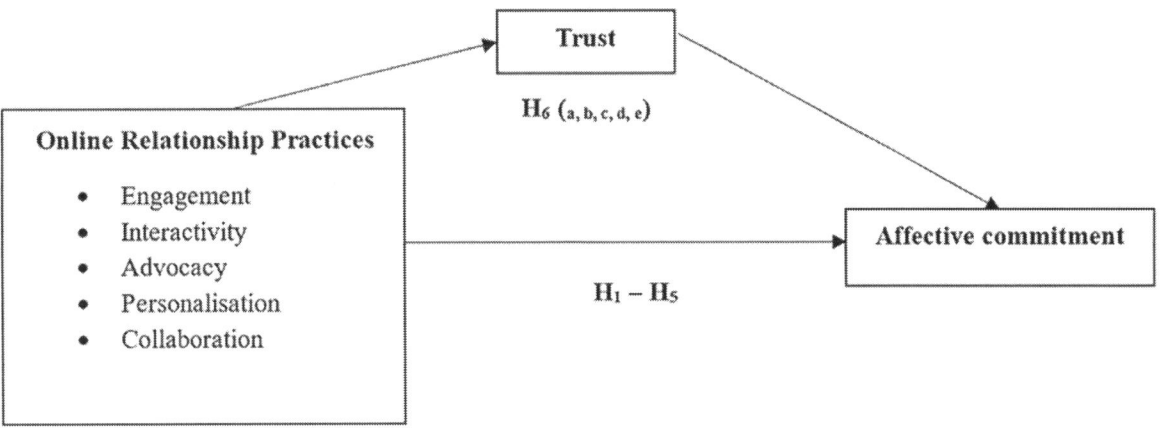

Chapter Summary

In this chapter readers were introduced to the basics of quantitative data analysis, the varieties of data analysis software that exist and the different types of data and variables there are. They further learned what goes into the selection of a specific data analysis technique to use in conducting research on a given phenomenon. Additionally, readers were introduced to the process of hypothesis formulation and testing. In the next chapter we will explore what goes into the selection of appropriate scale items and the design of a good questionnaire for the purposes of quantitative data collection.

Chapter Review

Question 1

Using examples of your choice, compare and contrast the types of variables?

Question 2

What are hypotheses and how do they relate with the research objectives and the research framework in any given research?

Question 3

What is Type I error and how does it differ from Type II error?

Chapter 2

Questionnaire Design

OBJECTIVES

This chapter seeks to provide readers with an in-depth understanding of questionnaire design. The learning outcome is to know how to design a good questionnaire for data collection, as well as how to capture various forms of data and design the structure of the questionnaire such that it enhances the collection of quantitative data.

WHY DESIGN A QUESTIONNAIRE?

For the purposes of collecting quantitative data, the survey method is often utilized. The survey method is relatively common in business and management research, and is regularly used to answer who, what, where, how much and how many questions.[8] It is often used in causal research and is designed to directly investigate the nature of respondents' thoughts, their opinions, as well as their feelings concerning a particular occurrence.[9] The survey method allows the researcher to collect quantitative data that can be quantitatively analyzed using descriptive and inferential statistics. To conduct a survey, a researcher needs to develop a collection of questions with answer options, often based on existing literature, in order to gather the information required from respondents. This collection of questions with answer options is what is referred to as a questionnaire. Questionnaires provide a fairly quick and efficient way of obtaining large amounts of information from a large number of respondents. The information can be collected relatively quickly because the researcher does not always need to be present when the questionnaires are being completed. This is very useful in situations where the population is quite large making individual interviews impractical.[10]

A well-designed questionnaire must:
1. Meet the requirements of the objectives of the research.
2. Be organized and worded to encourage respondents to provide accurate, unbiased and complete information.
3. Be arranged so that sound analysis and interpretation are possible.
4. Be brief and to the point
5. Be arranged such that the respondent(s) remains interested and engaged throughout providing their responses.

How to Design a Good Questionnaire

There are nine steps involved in designing a good questionnaire. These steps are discussed in the ensuing sections.

1. Decide the Information Required

To develop a good questionnaire, the researcher must first get properly acquainted with the topic and the area in which they desire to conduct the research. They must conduct a thorough literature review to establish a good understanding of the research in the area, especially those of the quantitative kind. This will give the researcher a fair idea of what work has been done on the same or similar topics in the past, what factors have not yet been examined, and how their study can build on what knowledge has already been discovered.[11] Research objectives and research hypotheses must also be formulated; based upon which the researcher will define the main information required in order to address the research objectives and test the study hypotheses.

2. Define the Target Respondents

Subsequently, the researcher must define the population about which he/she wishes to generalize from the sample data to be collected; which will lead them to develop a proper sampling frame (see Chapter 3).[11] They must also decide on the actual sample size of respondents they intend to survey for the study. Also, in designing the questionnaire it is important for the researcher to consider the characteristics of the target respondents, including factors such as their background and education level. The questionnaire must be adapted to the target respondents. This will go a long way to enhance the response rate of the survey.

3. Choose the Method(s) of Reaching your Target Respondents

The researcher must decide on how to access respondents to obtain their responses to the survey. There are several methods through which a researcher can contact potential respondents to obtain their responses to the survey, including self-completion, face-to-face, focus groups, postal or web surveys and telephone surveys. However, each method has its pros and cons. For instance, postal surveys can be relatively less expensive, but responses can be low and can take a long time to receive. Whereas, face-to-face surveys although quite expensive usually generates the more complete responses. Web surveys can also be cost-effective, but the response rates are largely inconsistent. Telephone surveys on the other hand can be costly, but will often generate high response rates, give fast turnaround and allow for further probing.[15] That being said, it is worthy to note that the method of contact will not only influence the nature of questions the researcher is able to ask as part of the questionnaire, but also the phrasing of the questions. The general rule is that the more sensitive or personal the information the researcher seeks to gather, the more personal the form of data collection should be.

4. Decide on Question Content

Researchers are often tempted to include various questions without critically assessing the relevance of these questions in addressing the objectives of the study. To curb the negative consequences of this practice, researchers must be prepared to ask themselves, "*Is this question really needed*?" In answering this question researchers will be guided to only include questions that give rise to data that will be of direct use in testing the research hypotheses formulated for the study. The content of the questions included in a questionnaire for a particular study are usually determined by the nature of the variables that they are purported to measure according to existing literature in the area under study. This is often presented in published work as a table of variables or items and their measures, as seen in Table 3. This indicates the specific variables, the individual items measuring them, as well as the sources of these measurement items.

TABLE 1 - TABLE OF ITEMS AND THEIR MEASURES[13]

CONSTRUCT	NUMBER OF ITEMS	ADAPTED FROM
Engagement	10 Items	Guo (2014); Cobos *et al.* (2009)
Interactivity	8 Items	Cobos *et al.* (2009), Farquhar and Rowley (2006)
Personalisation	8 Items	Guo (2014); Gan *et al.* (2007)
Collaboration	7 Items	Gan *et al.* (2007); Farquhar and Rowley (2006)
Online Trust	9 Items	Wang *et al.* (2015); Bilgihan and Bujisic (2015); Brun *et al.* (2014b); Hong and Cho (2011); Lee and Turban (2001)
Affective commitment	7 Items	Bilgihan and Bujisic (2015); Brun *et al.* (2014b); Dabholkar, van Dolen and de Ruyter (2009)
Calculative commitment	7 Items	Bilgihan and Bujisic (2015); Brun *et al.* (2014b); Dabholkar, van Dolen and de Ruyter (2009)
Normative commitment	7 Items	Brun *et al.* (2014b); Wallace *et al.* (2011); Jones *et al.* (2010)
Customer Loyalty	9 Items	Labrecque (2014), Bilgihan and Bujisic (2015); Huang and Shyu (2009); Liang *et al.* (2008)
Purchase Intention	6 Items	Ali (2016); Son *et al.* (2013)

Researchers are always encouraged to either adopt or adapt measurement items, often referred to as measurement scales, from existing literature on the subject matter when developing questionnaires for their research work. This enhances the reliability and validity of their measures. When a researcher **adopts** a measurement item or instrument, they take it verbatim as it is and apply it to their research, although there might be some minimal modifications required. However, in **adapting** a measurement item or instrument, the researcher significantly alters the instrument or measurement item to suit their unique circumstances. Thus, if in the course of conducting their literature review a researcher happens to find a pre-existing instrument or measurement item that will be useful to measure one or more variables in their study, they can either adopt or adapt it.[12] But, in cases where there are no pre-existing scales, the researcher has to develop them from scratch on the basis of literature.

5. Develop the Question Wording

At this point the researcher must decide the actual wording of the individual questions and measurement items to be included in the questionnaire. Here there are several things the researcher must take cognizance of. For instance, the researcher must always use words that respondents would understand and would naturally use themselves. They must avoid using terms in the question or response options that are open to wide interpretation. It is better for the researcher to use more specific and precise terms that will ensure that the interpretation ascribed to each question by respondents is much more precise and regular.[14] The researcher must further refrain from using technical jargons. The language of a questionnaire must be appropriate to the vocabulary of the population that is being studied.[17]

There are two main forms of survey questions: **Closed** and **Open-ended questions**.

1. *Closed Questions*

They are questions that have a limited number of responses, which the respondent is asked to choose from. These types of questions are standardized; such that all respondents are asked the same questions in the same order. This makes it easy for the questionnaire to be replicated and checked for reliability. Information obtained by this means can also be easily quantified, allowing for statistical analysis of the responses.[17] Closed questions structure respondents' answers by only allowing responses that fit into pre-determined options. These options can be based on categories that are restricted to as few as two options, i.e., *dichotomous* (e.g. 'yes' or 'no,' 'male' or 'female'), or include quite complex lists of alternatives from which the respondent can choose i.e. *polychotomous* (e.g. 'single, 'co-habiting', 'married', 'divorced', 'widowed'). Alternatively, they can be based on rankings, using a continuous rating scale of measurement, i.e. *Likert scale* (e.g. 'strongly disagree', 'disagree', 'neutral'. 'agree', 'strongly agree').

Likert scale is the most widely used approach to scaling responses in survey research. Named after its creator, Dr. Rensis Likert an American social scientist, the Likert scale is one of the most reliable ways to measure opinions, perceptions and behaviors. They are made up of questions that offer a range of answer options used to measure response levels from one extreme to another. As a rule, a Likert scale must always include a moderate or neutral midpoint. This is because neutral responses can prove to be valuable, in that they translate to the fact that the respondent does not have any opinion on the question.[18] Hence, all Likert scales have an 'odd' total number of points or response options, such as a 5-point Likert scale or a 7-point Likert scale. By providing an even number of response options, there is no option for neutrality. There are several response options available for Likert scale questions, depending on the objectives of the research to be conducted. For instance, there are scales that measure level of agreement (e.g. 'strongly disagree', 'disagree', 'neutral'. 'agree', 'strongly agree'); level of satisfaction (e.g. 'very dissatisfied', 'moderately dissatisfied', 'slightly dissatisfied', 'neutral', 'slightly satisfied', 'moderately satisfied', 'very satisfied') among others.

2. *Open-ended Questions*

These are questions that require the respondent to provide a free-form response in his/her own words. No pre-set response options are suggested. As such the respondents have the opportunity to answer the question in as much detail as they like, reflecting their true feelings on a topic. Open-ended questions enable the researcher to gather more in-depth answers from respondents. They often reveal the issues which are most important to the respondent, and this may lead to outcomes which were not originally anticipated when the survey was initiated. Therefore, they are often used for complex questions that cannot be answered in a few simple categories but require more detail and discussion. For instance, *'Can you provide your opinion on the current salary structure at your company?'*

Questionnaires often combine both closed and open-ended questions to gather data. The most common structure of a questionnaire is that the open-ended questions are placed at the latter section of the questionnaire, while the closed questions are placed at the beginning. This is because open-ended questions tend to require more thought and effort, and therefore take more time to answer than closed questions. In this case, the closed questions which are easier to answer must be placed at the first section, while the open-ended questions that require more thought are placed at the end of the questionnaire. This enhances the response of the questionnaire.

6. Put Questions into a Meaningful Order and Format

The appearance of a questionnaire can either enhance or diminish the quantity and quality of data collected. Research indicates that the way a respondent answers a questionnaire is largely determined by the order and format of the questions presented in the questionnaire.[14] Therefore, in designing a questionnaire, the researcher must be clear and concise. Opening questions should be easy to answer and not be in any way intimidating to respondents. This is because if they find the opening questions easy and pleasant to answer, they will be encouraged to continue. The questions should also progress logically from the least sensitive to the most sensitive, from behavioral to cognitive, as well as from the general to the more specific.[17] Questions on one aspect of a study, or one particular variable, should be grouped together. Respondents may feel it disconcerting to keep shifting from one aspect to another, or to be asked to return to some aspect of the study they think they have already given their opinions on. Nonetheless, the researcher must ensure that the most important items are not brought last, since some respondents may likely not complete the entire questionnaire.

7. Check the Length of the Questionnaire

In general, it is best for a questionnaire to be as short as possible. If the questionnaire gets too long the respondents' attention and commitment wane; making them open to the dangers of boredom and poorly considered, hurried responses, as well as interruptions by third parties.[14] Therefore, researchers must keep their questionnaires short and to the point. They must not be tempted to throw in additional questions, which are not relevant to their specific research objectives. If the questionnaire is too long, try to remove some questions by reading each question and asking yourself, 'Is this information relevant to my study?' If your answer is no, don't include it!

8. Pre-test the Questionnaire

At this point the questionnaire is just a draft. It is necessary to pre-test it with an initial sample of respondents before it is used in a full-scale survey. Begin by reading over the questionnaire and completing it as if you were a participant. While doing so, ask yourself 'Are the directions clear on how to respond?', 'Is the format appealing?' Likewise, read over each question looking for spelling and grammatical errors. These are to enable you identify and rectify any mistakes in the questionnaire before administering it to a larger test group. Once the questionnaire has been corrected and revised, it is time to pilot it. It is always a good idea to pre-test your survey questions with a small group of the intended respondents before you actually administer it on a large scale.[14] This will provide detailed and honest feedback to the researcher on whether or not the questions as they are worded will achieve the desired results, whether the questions have been placed in the best order, whether the questions are understood by all classes of respondent, whether additional or specifying questions are needed or whether some questions should be eliminated. Using the feedback from the pilot study the researcher can revise the questionnaire and go ahead to administer it among a larger sample. Nevertheless, if the changes required are quite extensive, the researcher needs to conduct a subsequent pilot study to ensure that the questionnaire is actually good enough for large scale administration.

9. Develop the Final Survey Form

Using the feedback from the pilot study the researcher makes final changes to the questionnaire. After these changes the researcher can go ahead to administer the questionnaire to the target sample of respondents.

QUESTIONNAIRE LAYOUT

This section delineates the general layout of a good questionnaire for survey research. This layout can be divided into three sections: *Part 1 – General Instructions*, *Part 2 – Background Information* and *Part 3 – Construct measures*.

Part 1 - General Instructions

The aim of this section is to attract and motivate your respondents and make them eager to participate. It does so by explaining the general objective of the survey to help the respondent to have a general understanding of the purpose of the research study. The requirements of the respondent's participation and other ethical considerations are also stated here indicating the confidentiality of participants' responses, as well as the use of the data gathered for purely academic and research purposes. Here the researcher can also give an indication as to how long it will take the respondent to complete the questionnaire. He/ she can then end the section by thanking the respondent for their participation.

Part 2 - Background Information

In this section, personal information about the background of the respondent is gathered. Data gathered in this section is mainly categorical in nature, including demographic information like gender, age, education level and marital status. Responses in this section are based on pre-determined dichotomous and polychotomous categories, such as 'male'/ 'female' or 'single', 'co-habiting', 'married', 'divorced', 'widowed'. Also, directions are provided here for respondents on how to answer the questions asked. Researchers must ensure that every item has an obvious place for each response to be indicated. Response categories should also be clearly described. Furthermore, every set of items that needs a different style of response requires for a new set of response directions to be provided for respondents.

Part 3 - Construct Measures

Data gathered in this section are mainly based on rankings, using a continuous rating scale of measurement, i.e. the Likert scale, such as 'strongly disagree', 'disagree', 'neutral'. 'agree', 'strongly agree' among others. Directions on how to respond to questions listed here are also provided for participants, as was done in the previous section. Participants need a general idea of what to expect for the items that they will soon be responding to. Thus, the researcher is expected to write a statement or two to prime them for what to expect with the subsequent items. An example of this is shown in Illustration 3; the following statement is included in Part 3 – Construct measures to provide direction to respondents. It reads, '**Please indicate the extent to which you agree or disagree with regard to your attitudes/ feelings about Online Relationship Marketing in the Ghanaian Banking Sector, using a scale of 1-5 where 1=Strongly Disagree, 2=Disagree, 3=Neutral, 4=Agree and 5=Strongly Agree**'. Ensure that the response categories in this section are consistent. Decide how points or options you want to include on your Likert scale and keep it consistent. Here, researchers must likewise ensure that every item has an obvious place for each response to be indicated. Response categories should also be clearly described. Furthermore, every set of items that needs a different style of response requires for a new set of response directions to be provided for respondents. Any open-ended questions pertaining to the study may also be included in this section.

Illustration 3 provides an example of a good questionnaire containing all the major sections described above to guide quantitative researchers in preparing their own.

Illustration 3 - Sample Questionnaire

Dear Sir/Madam,

I am a PhD candidate at the University of Ghana Business School. I am conducting a research on Online Relationship Marketing (ORM) and Customer Commitment in the Ghanaian banking industry. The study seeks to determine the impact of the online relationship marketing activities of Ghanaian banks through emails, social media and websites on customer commitment, trust and loyalty. Many thanks for taking a few minutes to answer this questionnaire. Please note that all information provided will be strictly confidential and will be used for academic purposes only. By completing the survey, you indicate that you voluntarily wish to participate in this research.

SECTION A: Background information (Please tick where appropriate)

1. **Gender:** a) Male [ ]   b) Female [ ]

2. **Age:** a) 18-20 [ ]   b) 21-30 [ ]   c) 31-40 [ ]   d) 41-50 [ ]   e) Above 50 [ ]

3. **Education Level:** a) Primary [ ] b) Secondary [ ] c) Tertiary - Undergraduate [ ]   d) Tertiary - Postgraduate Degree [ ] e) Diploma/ HND [ ] f) Others please specify……………

4. **Occupation:** a) Student [ ]   b) Salaried worker [ ]   c) Self-employed [ ]   d) Pensioner [ ]   e) Unemployed [ ]   f) Others please specify……………………

5. **Marital status:** a) Single [ ]   b) Cohabiting [ ]   c) Married [ ]   d) Separated [ ]   e) Divorced [ ]   f) Widowed [ ]

6. **Religion:** a) Christianity [ ]   b) Islam [ ]   c) Traditional religion [ ]   d) Others please specify………………

7. **Average monthly income:** a) Less than GHS 5,000 [ ]   b) GHS 5,000 – GHS 10,000 [ ]   c) GHS 11,000 – GHS 15,000 [ ]   d) Above GHS 15,000 [ ]

8. **Do you have a bank account?**   a) Yes [ ]   b) No [ ]

If you selected option (b) for Question 8, kindly return the questionnaire; otherwise kindly progress to Question 7.

9. **Online Activity**: Have you ever accessed your bank's online (internet) activities?
   a) Yes [   ]   b) No [   ]

10. **Online Relationship Channel:** Does your Bank use any of the following channels in communicating and interacting with you? (You may tick more than one).
    a) E-mail [   ]   b) Website [   ]   c) Social Media (Facebook/ Twitter) [   ]   d) None [   ]

11. **Name of the Bank -** Please provide the name of the bank which uses the email, website and/or social media to frequently communicate with you.

    ....

SECTION B: Perceptions about Online Relationship Marketing (ORM) in the Ghanaian Banking Sector.

Please indicate the extent to which you **agree** or **disagree** regarding your attitudes/ feelings about Online Relationship Marketing in the Ghanaian Banking Sector, using a scale of 1-5 where **1=Strongly Disagree**, **2=Disagree**, **3=Neutral, 4=Agree and 5=Strongly Agree.**

		Strongly Disagree	Disagree	Neutral	Agree	Strongly Agree
ORM ACTIVITIES						
12. Engagement						
i.	My bank's online platforms engage my attention	1	2	3	4	5
ii.	I write comments and messages on my bank's Facebook page	1	2	3	4	5
iii.	I contribute to conversations on my bank's Facebook page	1	2	3	4	5
iv.	My bank's website has a section for Frequently Asked Questions (FAQs)	1	2	3	4	5
v.	My bank's website displays banner advertisements for its products and services	1	2	3	4	5
vi.	My bank's website provides basic product information	1	2	3	4	5
vii.	I am able to make basic email enquiries to my bank	1	2	3	4	5
viii.	My bank has site navigation tools on their website	1	2	3	4	5
ix.	I 'like' content posted on my bank's Facebook page	1	2	3	4	5
x.	I retweet comments posted on my bank's Twitter handle	1	2	3	4	5

		Strongly Disagree	Disagree	Neutral	Agree	Strongly Agree
13. Interactivity						
i.	I can interact with my bank through their website	1	2	3	4	5
ii.	My bank's website has a search tool that enables me to locate items	1	2	3	4	5
iii.	I get the desired answers to my online enquiries	1	2	3	4	5
iv.	My bank's website has hotlinks to their Twitter/ Facebook pages	1	2	3	4	5
v.	I can interact with my bank through their Facebook page	1	2	3	4	5
vi.	24-hour live chat/ help is available on my bank's website	1	2	3	4	5
vii.	My bank promptly responds to my enquiries through email	1	2	3	4	5
viii.	My bank responds on time to my enquiries on Facebook	1	2	3	4	5
14. Personalisation						
i.	My name and personal information are always used by my bank in communicating with me online	1	2	3	4	5
ii.	My bank uses emails to send me personalized account information	1	2	3	4	5
iii.	My bank's website provides web page viewing in different languages	1	2	3	4	5
iv.	My bank offers a customer sign-in option on their website	1	2	3	4	5
v.	My bank's internet banking platform provides user authentication features	1	2	3	4	5
vi.	My bank's website makes me feel that I am a unique customer	1	2	3	4	5
vii.	My bank sends direct messages to me via Facebook	1	2	3	4	5
viii.	My bank's website makes service recommendations that match my needs	1	2	3	4	5
15. Collaboration						
i.	My bank's online platforms provide mechanisms that help me to evaluate and select appropriate products and services	1	2	3	4	5

		Strongly Disagree	Disagree	Neutral	Agree	Strongly Agree
ii.	Other customers provide helpful information on my bank's Facebook page	1	2	3	4	5
iii.	My bank's website and Facebook page allow me to upload information and feedback regarding their products and services	1	2	3	4	5
iv.	My bank offers exclusive webpages and information for customers on their website	1	2	3	4	5
v.	My bank has downloadable documents and brochures for customers (e.g. financial statements, security tips) on their website	1	2	3	4	5
vi.	There are value adding features (e.g. currency converter; foreign exchange rates) on my bank's website	1	2	3	4	5
vii.	My bank has a community on Facebook to facilitate communication among customers	1	2	3	4	5
16. ONLINE TRUST						
i.	I can count on my bank to ensure that transactions carried out on its website are without error	1	2	3	4	5
ii.	I think that the information presented on my bank's website is reliable	1	2	3	4	5
iii.	I believe that my bank will not distribute my personal information without my permission	1	2	3	4	5
iv.	My bank tries to be fair in dealing with all its customers online	1	2	3	4	5
v.	My bank keeps customers' best interests in mind	1	2	3	4	5
vi.	My bank makes every effort to address and solve customer concerns and problems online	1	2	3	4	5
vii.	I think that my bank would not do anything intentional on their website that would be unfair to customers	1	2	3	4	5
viii.	My bank provides features on their website (e.g. a Web form; contact center) that allow me to report security vulnerabilities	1	2	3	4	5

		Strongly Disagree	Disagree	Neutral	Agree	Strongly Agree
ix.	I feel like my privacy is protected while transacting with my bank online.	1	2	3	4	5

COMMITMENT

17. Affective commitment

		Strongly Disagree	Disagree	Neutral	Agree	Strongly Agree
i.	I feel an emotional attachment to my bank	1	2	3	4	5
ii.	Being able to transact with my bank means a lot to me	1	2	3	4	5
iii.	I feel a strong sense of belonging with my bank	1	2	3	4	5
iv.	I am proud to transact with my bank	1	2	3	4	5
v.	I enjoy discussing the good aspects of my bank with other people	1	2	3	4	5
vi.	It is easy to become attached to my bank	1	2	3	4	5
vii.	I enjoy the relationship that I have formed with my bank	1	2	3	4	5

18. Calculative Commitment

		Strongly Disagree	Disagree	Neutral	Agree	Strongly Agree
i.	It would be very difficult for me to stop using my bank's website	1	2	3	4	5
ii.	The management of my personal finances would be disrupted if I decided to stop patronizing my bank's services	1	2	3	4	5
iii.	I think that the cost in time, money and effort to switch to another bank is high	1	2	3	4	5
iv.	I am afraid something will be lost if I stop using my bank	1	2	3	4	5
v.	Some aspects of my life will be affected if I cease patronizing my bank	1	2	3	4	5
vi.	It would save me time if I stay with my bank	1	2	3	4	5
vii.	There are no banking services comparable to those offered by my bank	1	2	3	4	5

19. Normative commitment

		Strongly Disagree	Disagree	Neutral	Agree	Strongly Agree
i.	I feel an obligation to patronize my bank's services	1	2	3	4	5

		Strongly Disagree	Disagree	Neutral	Agree	Strongly Agree
ii.	I am obligated to maintain a relationship with my bank	1	2	3	4	5
iii.	It is my duty to transact with my bank	1	2	3	4	5
iv.	I would feel guilty if I left my bank right	1	2	3	4	5
v.	Even if it were to my advantage, I do not feel it would be right to leave my bank right now	1	2	3	4	5
vi.	My bank deserves my continued patronage	1	2	3	4	5
vii.	I owe a great deal of gratitude to my bank	1	2	3	4	5
20. CUSTOMER LOYALTY						
i.	I will encourage friends and relatives to use the services of my bank	1	2	3	4	5
ii.	I will recommend my bank to anyone who seeks banking advice	1	2	3	4	5
iii.	I would be willing to pay a higher price for my bank's services over other banks	1	2	3	4	5
iv.	I prefer my bank to its competitors	1	2	3	4	5
v.	My bank is the best bank for me	1	2	3	4	5
vi.	I will say positive things about my bank to others	1	2	3	4	5
vii.	I will continue to deal with my bank into the future	1	2	3	4	5
viii.	I would be willing to defend my bank in the face of any controversy	1	2	3	4	5
ix.	I would consider my bank as my first choice for patronizing banking services	1	2	3	4	5
21. PURCHASE INTENTION						
i.	I would always do business with my bank	1	2	3	4	5
ii.	I would continue to do business with my bank in the coming months	1	2	3	4	5
iii.	I consider my bank as my first choice for future transactions	1	2	3	4	5
iv.	Given the chance, I would consider purchasing my bank's services in the future	1	2	3	4	5
v.	I intend to keep patronizing my bank's services	1	2	3	4	5

	Strongly Disagree	Disagree	Neutral	Agree	Strongly Agree
vi. I am glad to patronize my bank's services	1	2	3	4	5

Additional Questions:

Please kindly provide any relevant general comments about your bank's relationship with you.

_____
_____
_____
_____
_____

Please kindly provide any relevant general comments about your bank's website.

_____
_____
_____
_____
_____

Thank you very much

Chapter Summary

In this chapter, readers learned how to design a good questionnaire to facilitate their quantitative data collection. They learned how to formulate questions in order to appropriately capture respondent information, as well as how to outline the various sections of the questionnaire to expedite the data collection process. The ensuing chapter discusses the rubrics of sampling, delving into the various sampling procedures and how they are conducted.

Chapter Review

Question 1

Briefly discuss the key characteristics of a good questionnaire.

Chapter 3

Sampling

OBJECTIVES

This chapter seeks to introduce readers to the various sampling techniques available and how they can use them to obtain samples that are representative of their research population. The chapter further introduces readers to various quantitative formulae with which they can calculate the appropriate sample size for their study.

SELECTING A SAMPLE

Sampling is a process used in data analysis in which a predetermined number of observations are selected from a larger population. The methodology used to sample from a larger population depends mainly on the objectives of the study and the type of analysis that is being performed. Sampling is an important aspect of any research, given that the sample of a study can have a profound effect on the outcome of a study. In sampling, it is assumed that samples are drawn from the population, and that the sample means and population means are equal. A **population** can be defined as a complete set that includes all the cases, individuals, institutions, or entities that are the object of a research investigation. However, gathering information from an entire population will be time consuming and costly. Therefore, instead we make inferences about the population with the help of a sample.[19] But, once the researcher has identified the population for the study, there is the need for them to determine the sampling frame for the study before they can actually draw out a sample. The **sampling frame** refers to the complete list of the population obtained by the researcher from which he/ she will draw their final sample. There are two main types of sampling techniques available to researchers: **Probability or Representative sampling** and **Non-probability or Judgmental sampling**.[8] These are discussed as follows.

Probability or Representative Sampling

Probability or Representative sampling is a group of sampling techniques in which units are selected from the population at random using probabilistic methods. This enables researchers to make statistical inferences and generalizations from the resultant sample to the population of interest.[22] Probability sampling techniques include **Simple random sampling**, **Systematic sampling**, *Stratified* **random sampling** and **Cluster sampling**. These are explained in the next sections.

Simple Random Sampling

Simple random sampling involves the random selection of the sample from the sampling frame, such that each case has the same probability of being chosen as any other case. It involves numbering each of the cases in the sampling frame with a unique number and selecting cases using random numbers until the actual sample size is reached.[8] Simple random sampling is best utilized when the researcher has an accurate and easily accessible sampling frame that lists the entire population. This enables researchers to obtain samples that are usually representative of the population.

Systematic Sampling

Systematic sampling involves the selection of the sample at regular intervals from the sampling frame. Here, each of the cases in the sampling frame is identified with a unique number. The first case is then selected using a random number, then subsequent cases are selected systematically using the sampling fraction to determine the frequency of selection. The *sampling fraction* is the actual sample size divided by the total population. It represents the proportion of the total population that the researcher needs to select. For instance, if the sampling fraction is 1/5 the researcher will need to select every fifth case from the sampling frame. However, sometimes the calculation results in a more complicated fraction; when this occurs, it is normally acceptable to round the population down to the nearest 10 (or 100) and to increase the minimum sample size until a simpler sampling fraction can be calculated.[8]

Stratified Random Sampling

This form of probability sampling involves dividing the population into homogeneous subgroups and then taking a simple random sample in each subgroup. However, it is only possible to do this if you are aware of, and can easily distinguish, significant strata in your sampling frame. This type of sampling is relevant because sometimes the researcher may be interested in particular strata or groups within the population. Therefore, with the stratified sample, there is an equal chance (probability) of selecting each unit from within a particular stratum or group. This ensures representation from not only the overall population, but also all the key subgroups of interest to the researcher within the population, especially small minority groups. If the researcher wishes to be able to talk about subgroups, this may be the only way to effectively do so.[20] For instance, if the aim is to obtain a stratified sample of an organization's employees based on their salary grade, we must divide the sampling frame into discrete salary grades (strata), number each of the cases within each salary grade (stratum) with a unique number and then select the sample using either simple random or systematic sampling, as discussed earlier.[8]

Cluster Sampling

Cluster sampling shares some amount of similarity with stratified sampling, given that the researcher is required to divide the population into discrete groups prior to sampling. However, in this form of sampling the groups are referred to as clusters and can be based on any naturally occurring grouping.[8] Selection of the sample is done by randomly selecting specific clusters and including all the members from these clusters. Thus, the overall sample consists of every member from some of the clusters, which are selected at random.[21]

Non-probability Sampling

Non-probability sampling techniques are a range of sampling techniques that enable researchers to select samples based on their subjective judgment. Hence, subjective methods are used to decide which elements should be included in the sample. Techniques available under this umbrella of techniques include **Purposive sampling**, **Quota sampling**, **Snowball sampling** and **Convenience sampling**, as discussed in the ensuing sections.

Purposive Sampling or Judgmental Sampling

In this approach to sampling the researcher selects the sample with a 'purpose' in mind. It enables the researcher to use his/ her expert judgment to select cases that will best enable them to address their research objectives. This form of sampling is often used when working with very small samples such as in case study research, which is primarily qualitative. However, it can also be used in quantitative studies where the researcher wishes to select cases that will be particularly informative for their study.[8]

Quota Sampling

Under this form of non-probability sampling the aim is to end up with a sample that contains strata (groups) that are proportional to those of interest to the researcher in the population being studied. Suitable cases are added until the required quota or number is achieved. In proportional quota sampling you want to represent the major characteristics of the population by sampling a proportional amount of each. For example, if you know the population has 40% women and 60% men, and you want a total sample size of 100, you will sample using this ratio until you get those percentages in your final sample. So, if you have already got the 40 women for your sample, but not the sixty men, you will continue to sample men and even if legitimate women respondents come along, you will not sample them because you have already met your "quota" for women.[20]

Convenience Sampling

Convenience sampling enables the researcher to select a sample based on their accessibility and proximity to the researcher. It differs from purposive sampling in that expert judgment is not used to select a representative sample of elements. Here, individual cases are sampled mainly because they are *'convenient'* sources of data. This technique is particularly suitable in instances where the population is so large that it is simply impossible to include every individual in the sampling frame.

Snowball Sampling

In snowball sampling, the researcher begins by identifying an entity that meets the criteria for inclusion in their study. They then ask them to recommend others who they may know who also meet the same criteria for inclusion in the study. In doing so selected group members identify additional members to be included in the sample for the study. This method of sampling is quite useful when the target population for the study are either inaccessible or hard to reach. Although this method may not always lead to representative samples, there are times when it may be the best sampling approach available.[20] Let's assume a researcher was conducting a study on the parents of children with autism. It is unlikely that they will be able to find a complete list of parents with autistic children within a particular geographical area. However, if they were to go to that area and identify one or two parents with such children, they may find that these parents can link them to parents in their vicinity with similar circumstances and even tell them how they can contact them.

DETERMINING APPROPRIATE SAMPLE SIZE

Determining an appropriate sample size for a quantitative study is not an easy task. There are a number of factors that the researcher has to consider, including the generalizability of their findings to the study population, as well as the amount of sampling error involved in conducting the research. By using a sample in conducting a study, the outcomes of the study become susceptible to some degree of uncertainty, since the researcher cannot prove with 100% certainty that their findings based on the sample are a true representation of the entire general population. This uncertainty is referred to as the **sampling error** or **margin of error** and is measured by means of a **confidence interval**. The general rule pertaining to acceptable margins of error in educational and social research differ, depending on the specific sample size calculation formula being used. For instance, according to Cochran[25], who distinguishes between the calculation of sample sizes for research focusing on either continuous or categorical data. Thus, the acceptable margin of error for categorical data, differs significantly from the acceptable margin of error for continuous data, as we will observe shortly. However, this is mainly dependent on which type of variable is playing a primary role in the study. Literature indicates that samples of a larger size are more likely to be representative of the population from which they are drawn than smaller samples.[8] Therefore, to arrive at an appropriate sample size that is sufficiently large, certain mathematical formulae have been suggested that can be used in the calculation, depending on what the researcher knows about the population. There are many formulae that a researcher can adopt but the most popular among these are:

i. **Taro Yamane's Formula for Sample Size**[26]
ii. **Cochran's Sample Size Formula**[25]

Taro Yamane's Formula for Sample Size

Yamane[26] provides a simplified formula for researchers to calculate sample sizes. The formula for the ideal sample size according to Yamane[26] for infinite populations, is given as:

$$n = \frac{N}{1+N(e)^2}, \text{where}$$

N is population size, **n** is the resulting sample size and **e** is the level of precision. In order to effectively calculate the actual sample size, using this formula, the researcher must go through the following steps.

Step 1: Decide on the individual parameters based on the requirements of the formula. These normally include:

i. *Population size* - Don't worry if you are unsure about this number. It is common for the population size to be either unknown or approximated.[24]

ii. *Level of precision* - This is represented by a confidence interval of **+/- 5% (0.05), +/- 7% (0.07) and +/- 10% (0.10)** depending on the researcher's desired level of precision.

Step 2: Insert your parameters into the formula.

Step 3: Round off your answer to a whole number, since you cannot sample a fraction of a unit.

Illustration 4

Calculate the sample size for a population of 2000 units, assuming a precision level of +/-7%.

Solution

Using Yamane[26]'s formula for sample size, **N** = 2000 units, **n** = sample size, **e** = 0.07. Given these values, the sample size is calculated as follows:

$$n = \frac{2000}{1+2000(0.07)^2} = 185$$

This gives an acceptable sample size of not less than 185 respondents.

Cochran's Sample Size Formula

Cochran[25] provides a slightly more complex formula for researchers to calculate sample sizes. This formula is unique in the sense that it delineates the computation of the ideal sample size for infinite populations in studies where continuous data is the main focus and categorical variables do not play a primary role, from studies in which categorical data is the main focus and continuous variables do not play a primary role. The formula is given as:

$$n = \frac{(t)^2 * (s)^2}{(e)^2}$$, where

n is the resulting sample size, *t* is the Z-score value that corresponds to the researcher's selected alpha level, *s* represents the estimate of variance in the population depending on the type of variable, whether categorical or continuous that is playing a primary role in the study and *e* is the acceptable margin of error, also depending on which type of variable, whether categorical or continuous is playing a primary role in the study. In order to effectively calculate the actual sample size using this formula, the researcher must go through the following steps.

Step 1: Decide on the individual parameters based on the requirements of the formula. These normally include:

i. *Alpha level (significance level)* - The most common alpha levels used here are **0.1** (90% confidence level), **0.05** (95% confidence level) and **0.01** (99% confidence level). Each alpha level corresponds to a particular ***t* value (Z-score),** this is a constant value needed for the equation.
   a. *0.1* – t value (Z-score) = *1.645*
   b. *0.05* – t value (Z-score) = *1.96*
   c. *0.01* – t value (Z-score) = *2.576*

ii. *Estimate of variance in the population* - For continuous data, this is estimated as the number of points on the Likert scale and divided by the number of standard deviations that would include all the possible values in the range. For example, if a researcher used a 5-point Likert scale, given that 4 standard deviations (4 to each side of the mean) would capture 98% of all responses, the calculations would be as follows: **5** divided by **4 = 1.25**. But, when estimating the variance of a categorical data, involving dichotomous variables such as gender, it is recommended that researchers use **0.50** as the estimate of variance. This proportion will result in the maximum sample size.

iii. *Acceptable margin of error* - This is represented by a confidence interval of **+/- 0.05** for categorical data and **+/- 0.03 x the number of points on the Likert scale** for continuous data, depending on which type of variable, whether categorical or continuous is playing a primary role in the study; as mentioned at the beginning of the section. The absolute value without the +/- sign is what is entered into the formula.

Step 2: Insert your parameters into the formula.

Step 3: Round off your answer to a whole number, since you cannot sample a fraction of a unit.

Illustration 5

Calculate the sample size for a population of 2000 units, assuming continuous data where a categorical variable does not play a primary role with an alpha value of 0.05.

Solution

Using Cochran (1977)'s formula for sample size, n = sample size, t = 1.96, assuming a 95% confidence level, s = 1.25, assuming a 5-point Likert scale and e = 0.15 assuming that continuous data is playing a primary role. Given these values, the sample size is calculated as follows:

$$n = \frac{(1.96)^2 * (1.25)^2}{(0.15)^2} = 300$$

This gives an acceptable sample size of not less than 300 respondents.

Chapter Summary

This chapter exposed readers to the various sampling techniques available, mainly Probability and Non-probability sampling techniques, and how they can be used to obtain representative samples for their research. Readers further learned how to differentiate between the various probability and non-probability sampling techniques, as well as estimate the appropriate sample size for their study using some mathematical formulae. The next chapter will delve into descriptive statistics and their role in quantitative data analysis.

Chapter Review

Question 1

Calculate the sample size for a population of 10,000 students, assuming continuous data where a categorical variable does not play a primary role with an alpha value of 0.05 assuming a 7 point Likert scale.

....

....

....

....

....

....

....

Question 2

Calculate the sample size for a population of 5000 units, assuming a precision level of +/- 5%.

....

....

....

....

....

....

....

Chapter 4

Descriptive Statistics

OBJECTIVES

In this chapter readers will learn about descriptive statistics and how they can be used to describe and compare the basic characteristics of their sample and data set. They will further learn about the different types of descriptive statistics, along with a practical demonstration of how to derive them using SPSS software.

What are Descriptive Statistics?

Descriptive statistics are used to describe the basic features of the data in a given study. They provide simple summaries about the sample and the measures in the survey. Coupled with some simple graphics, they form the basis of virtually every quantitative data analysis. Descriptive statistics are used to present quantitative descriptions of a data set in a manageable form, enabling us to reduce large amounts of data into a simpler summary. Conducting a descriptive statistical analysis of a data set is absolutely essential, as it provides a lot of valuable insights about data. There are three major characteristics of variables in a data set that we consider under descriptive statistics. These are the distribution, the central tendency and the dispersion of each variable. There are measures for each of these characteristics, which are subsequently explained, including:

1. Frequency Distribution
2. Measures of Central Tendency
3. Measures of Dispersion

Frequency Distribution

The frequency distribution is a summary of the frequency of individual values for a variable(s) in a given study. The simplest distribution would list every value of a variable and the number of respondents who selected or responded on each value. This can be calculated for both categorical and continuous data. Depending on the particular type of variable (categorical or continuous), all of the data values may be represented, or they may be grouped into categories. For example, a frequency distribution would describe gender by listing the number of and/or percentage of males and females in the overall data set. This is very helpful for researchers when it comes to detecting missing values in a given data set. Frequency distributions can be portrayed in two ways, either in the form of a table or as a graph (e.g. Bar chart, pie chart or histogram).[27]

Measures of Central Tendency

A measure of central tendency is a single value that attempts to describe a set of data by identifying the central position within that data set. It is an estimate of the center point of a distribution of values. There are three main measures of central tendency, namely the **Mode**, **Median** and **Mean**.

Mode

The mode is the most frequently occurring value in the set of scores for a given item in the data set.[27] Although, it is the only measure of central tendency that can be calculated and sensibly interpreted for both categorical and continuous data. However, even though the remaining two measures of central tendency are mainly suitable for continuous data, most statistical analysis software will also calculate them for categorical data if they have been coded numerically.[8]

Median

The median is the score found at the exact middle of the set of values. It is the middle score for a set of values in a data set that have been arranged in order of magnitude.[27] For variables that have an even number of data values, the median will occur halfway between the two middle data values.[8]

Mean

The mean, also known as the average is relatively the most commonly used measure of central tendency.[27] It is computed by adding up all the individual values under a particular item and dividing it by the number of values.

Measures of Dispersion

Measures of dispersion indicate the spread of the values around the central tendency of a given data set.[27] To describe this spread, there are a number of statistics available to researchers, including the range, quartiles, variance and standard deviation. But, the two commonly used measures are the **Range** and the **Standard deviation**, which are subsequently explained. Like the measures of central tendency, although measures of dispersion are mainly suitable for only continuous data, most statistical analysis software will also calculate them for categorical data if they have been coded numerically.[8]

Range

The range refers to the difference between the highest and lowest values for a given item in a data set. It is the simplest measure of spread, which makes it relatively easy for the researcher to spot any possible outliers in a given data set.[8]

Standard deviation (SD)

The standard deviation is a figure that is used to tell how the values for an individual item are spread out from the mean in a data set. In comparison to the range it is a more accurate and detailed estimate of dispersion that makes it easier for a researcher to spot outliers. This is because an outlier can greatly exaggerate the range.[27] Standard deviation can never be a negative number, due to the way it's calculated. The formula for standard deviation is computed using squares of the individual values. Thus, the square of a number cannot be negative; even two negative numbers when they are squared become positive. Furthermore, standard deviation measures distance from the mean and distances are never negative numbers.[28] A small standard deviation means that the values in a statistical data set are close to the mean of the data set, on average, and a large standard deviation means that the values in the data set are farther away from the mean, on average. The smallest possible value for a standard deviation is 0, and that happens only in contrived situations where every single number in the data set is exactly the same (indicating no deviation/ spread).

PRACTICAL DEMONSTRATION

A researcher run a survey among 600 retail bank customers. Her objective was to ascertain the **gender** (categorical variable) of each retail bank customer to know how many were male and how many were female; as well as whether or not there were more males than females. Also, she wanted to find out their average response to the statement, '*My bank promptly responds to my enquiries through email*', which was captured in the survey as **Int7** (continuous variable) and measured on a scale of 1-5 where 1=Strongly Disagree, 2=Disagree, 3=Neutral, 4=Agree and 5=Strongly Agree (i.e., these are the two constructs we are interested in).

Procedure in SPSS

1. Click **Analyze** > **Descriptive Statistics** > **Frequencies** on the top menu, as shown below:

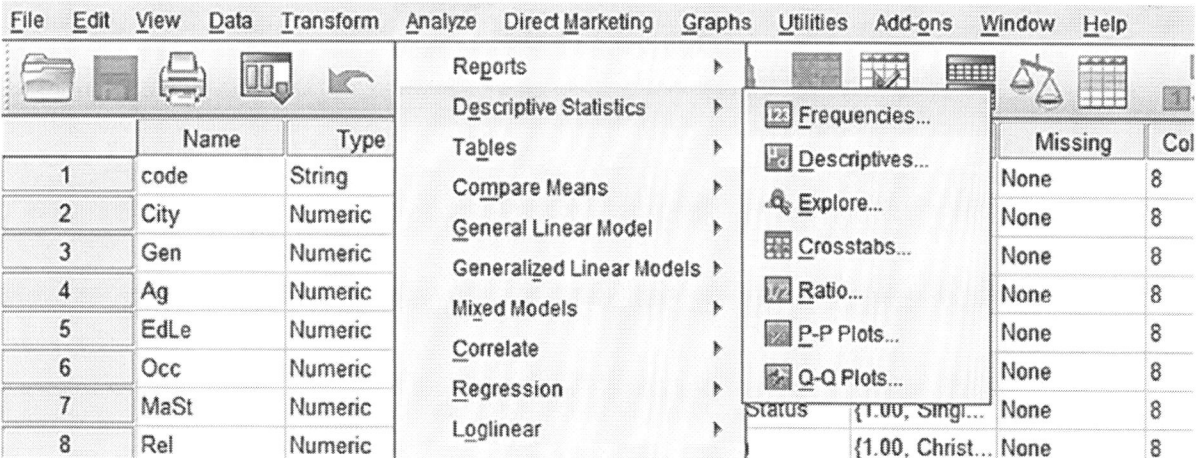

2. You will be presented with the **Frequencies** dialogue box, as shown below:

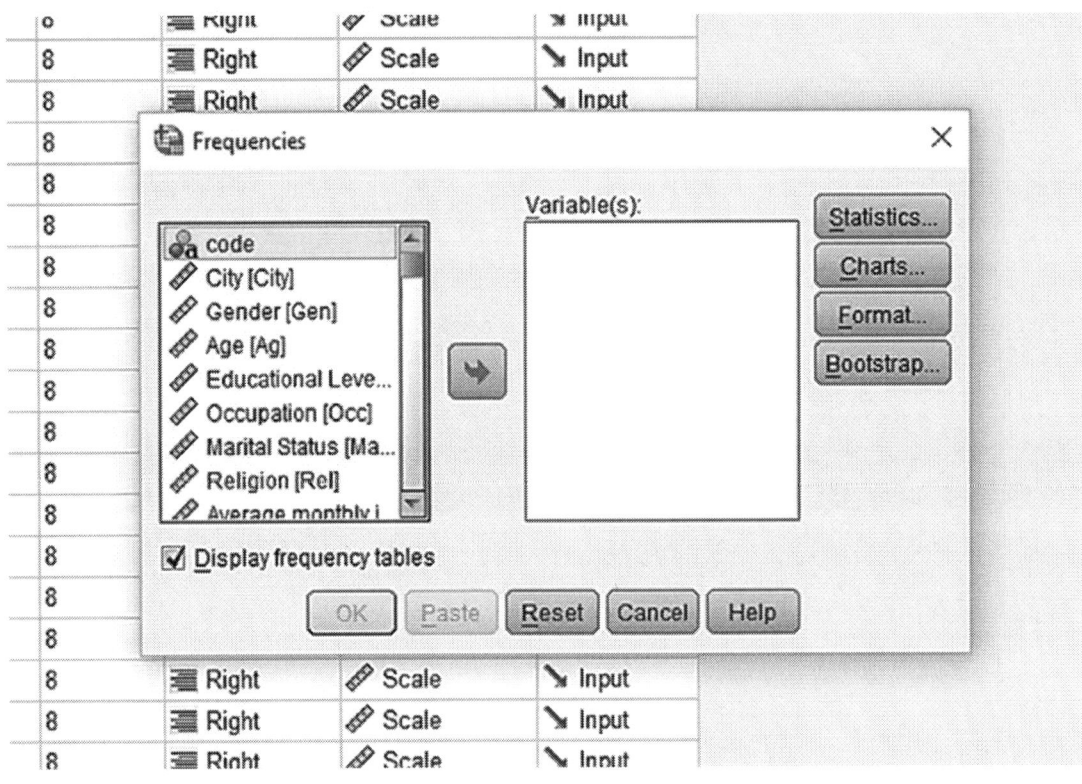

3. Transfer the variables that need to be tested for descriptive statistics into the **Variable(s)** box by either dragging-and-dropping or using the arrow button. In this example, we transfer the Gender variable and Int7 into the **Variable(s)** box. You will then be presented with the following screen:

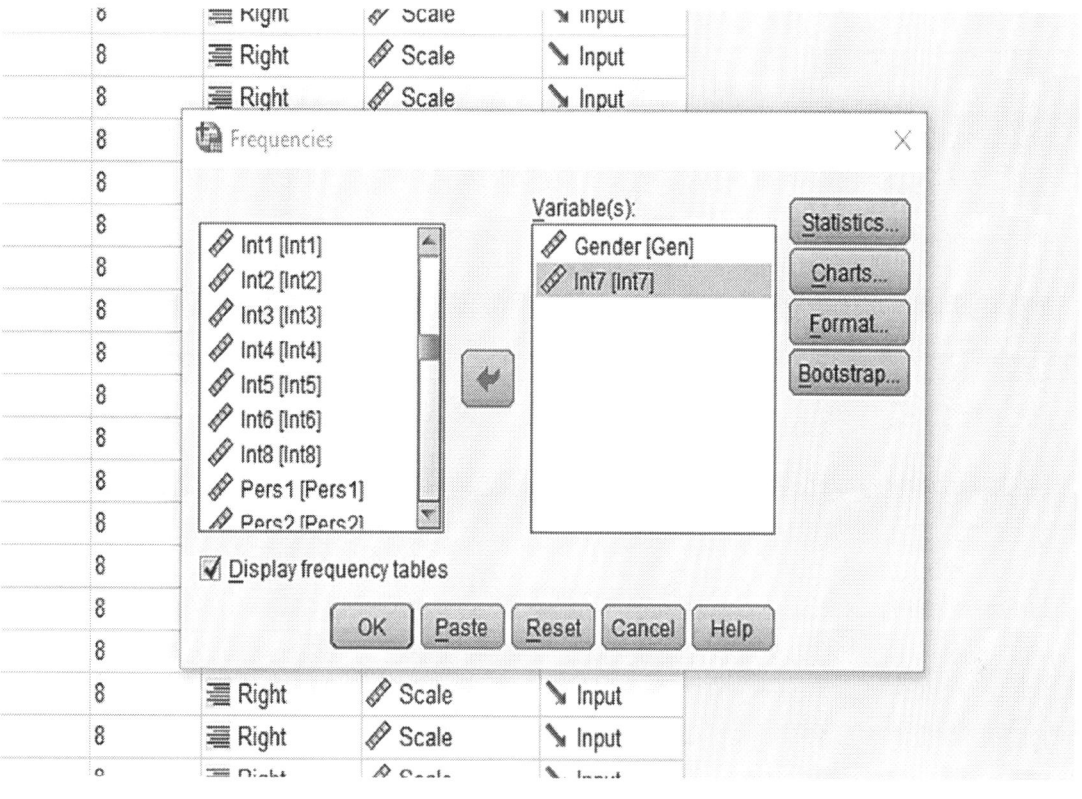

4. Click the **Statistics** button. You will be presented with the **Frequencies: Statistics** dialogue box, as shown below. Select **Mean**, **Median**, **Mode**, **Std. deviation** and **Range**. Click **Continue**.

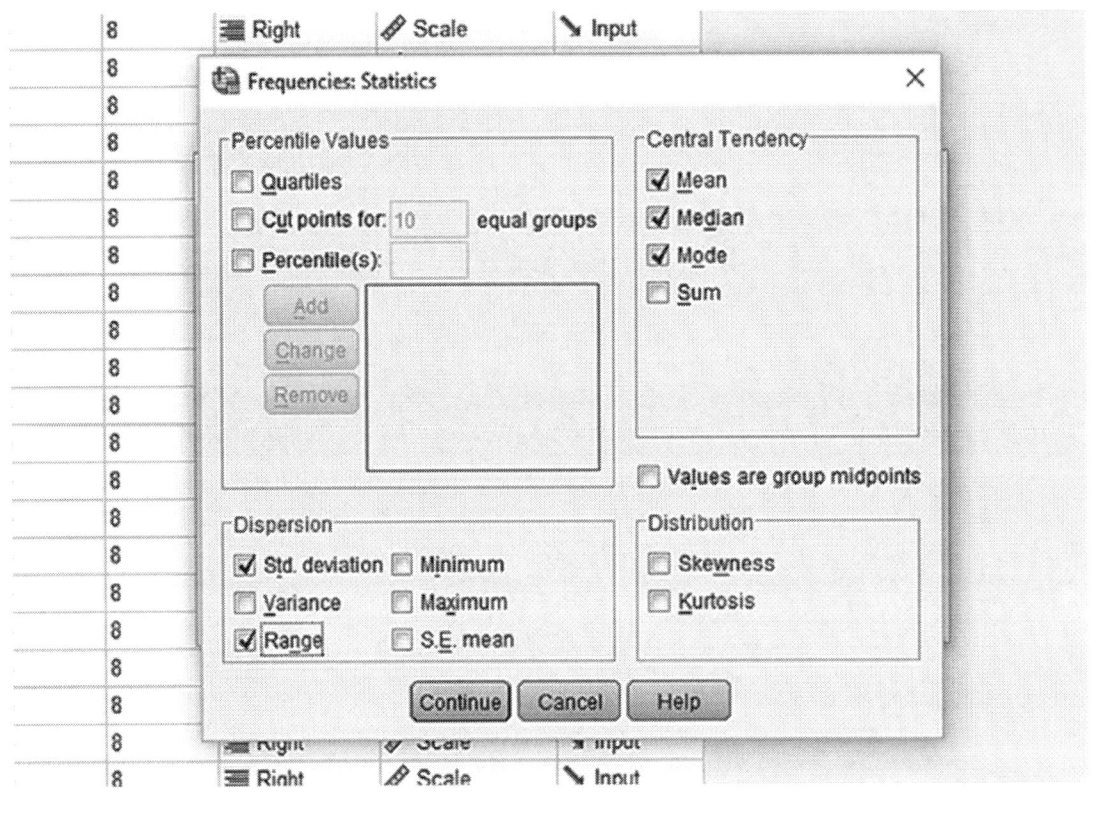

5. Click the **Charts** button. You will be presented with the **Frequencies: Charts** dialogue box, as shown below. Select the preferred Chart Type and the preferred Chart values.

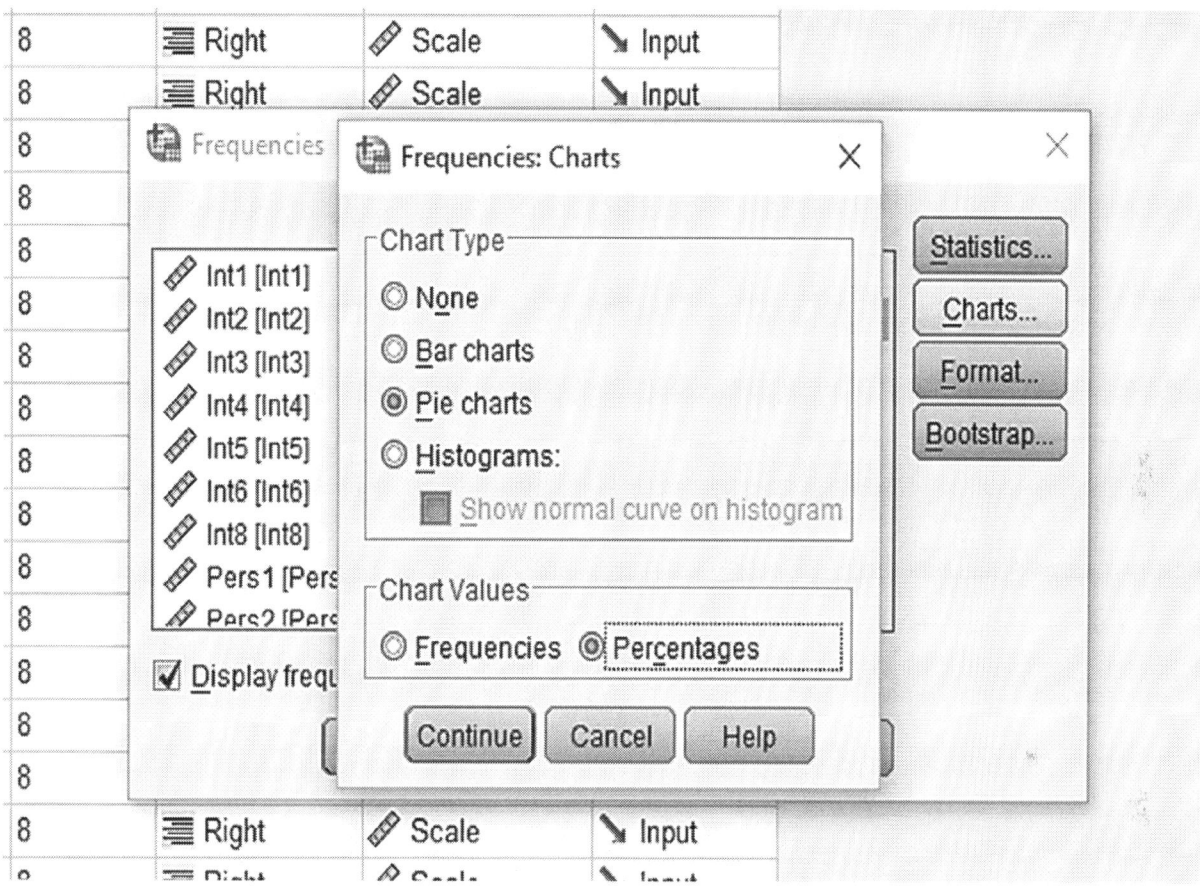

6. Click the **Continue** button and then click **OK** to view the output.

SPSS Output Required

The output generated by SPSS Statistics can provide a lot of information about your analysis, including identifying missing values in the data set, as seen below.

Statistics

		Gender	Int7
N	Valid	600	600
	Missing	0	0
Mean		1.3883	3.5483
Median		1.0000	4.0000
Mode		1.00	4.00
Std. Deviation		.48778	1.25975
Range		1.00	4.00

Frequency Table

Gender

		Frequency	Percent	Valid Percent	Cumulative Percent
Valid	Male	367	61.2	61.2	61.2
	Female	233	38.8	38.8	100.0
	Total	600	100.0	100.0	

Int7

		Frequency	Percent	Valid Percent	Cumulative Percent
Valid	Strongly Disagree	89	14.8	14.8	14.8
	Disagree	15	2.5	2.5	17.3
	Neutral	93	15.5	15.5	32.8
	Agree	284	47.3	47.3	80.2
	Strongly Agree	119	19.8	19.8	100.0
	Total	600	100.0	100.0	

Pie Chart

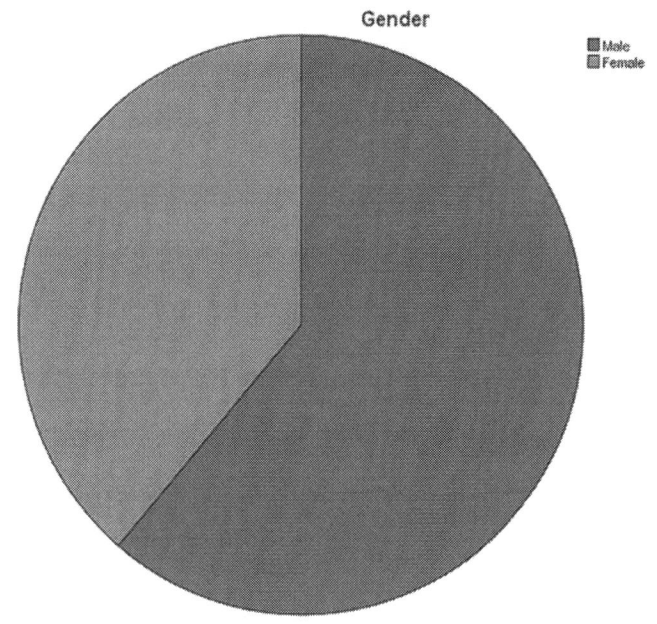

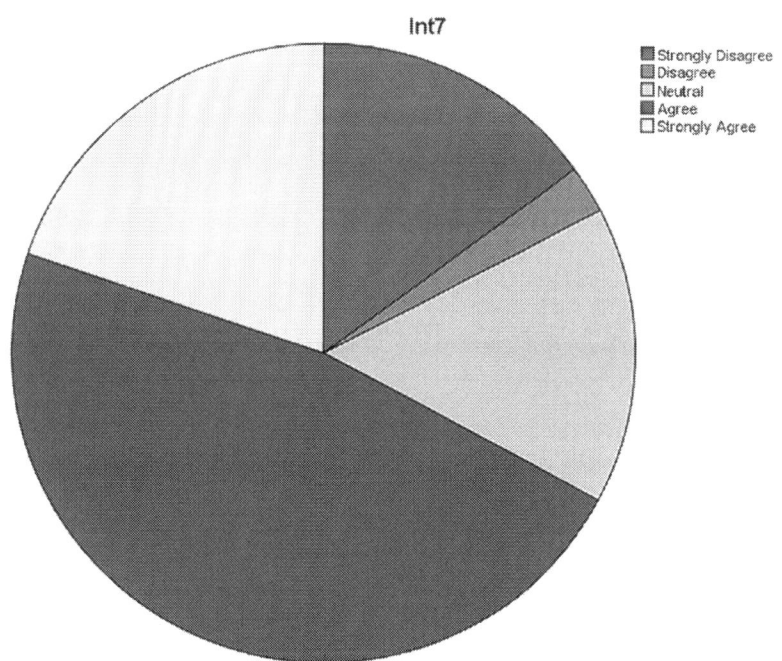

Chapter Review

Questions

In reference to the SPSS Output in this chapter, answer the following

1. Check the range and standard deviation values for both variables. Do these make sense; explain how? Do they indicate the presence of any outliers?
2. Check the mean score for both variables. Do these make sense; explain how?
3. Check the mode and median for both variables. Do these make sense; explain how?

Presentation of Output

Typically, in presenting quantitative analysis in a thesis or research article, there are certain descriptive statistics that are required, depending on the area of research and the topic being researched. Illustration 6 shows examples of descriptive statistics for categorical and continuous variables presented as part of a study on Online Relationship Marketing conducted for an academic thesis.[13]

Illustration 6 - Profile of Respondents

This illustration shows the descriptive statistics of the demographic data (categorical data) of a sample of respondents. It also shows the descriptive statistics of specific variables measured in the survey (continuous data). The descriptive statistics presented in Table 2 relate to the gender, age and educational level (categorical variables) for a total of 429 respondents.[13] Nonetheless, the researcher can add as many other categorical variables if necessary. This information can also be depicted in the form of a graph for each of the items as shown in Figure 3. This type of graph is known as a pie chart, but SPSS offers other graph options including bar charts and histograms, as seen in the SPSS procedure above. The descriptive statistics for the measurement items of two variables, interactivity and engagement (continuous variables) are presented in Table 3 along with their means and standard deviations. Researchers are however free to include other measures of dispersion and central tendency for additional continuous variables, if the requirements of the study call for it.

TABLE 2 - PROFILE OF RESPONDENTS

Demographic Profile	Number of Respondents (*N* = 429)	Valid Percentage (%)
Gender		
Male	272	63.4
Female	157	36.6
Age		
18-20	2	0.5
21-30	121	28.2
31-40	182	42.4
41-50	97	22.6
Above 50	27	6.3
Educational Level		
Primary	5	1.2
Secondary	137	31.9
Tertiary-Undergraduate	103	24.0
Tertiary-Postgraduate	38	8.9
Diploma/ HND	146	34.0

FIGURE 3 - AGE OF RESPONDENTS

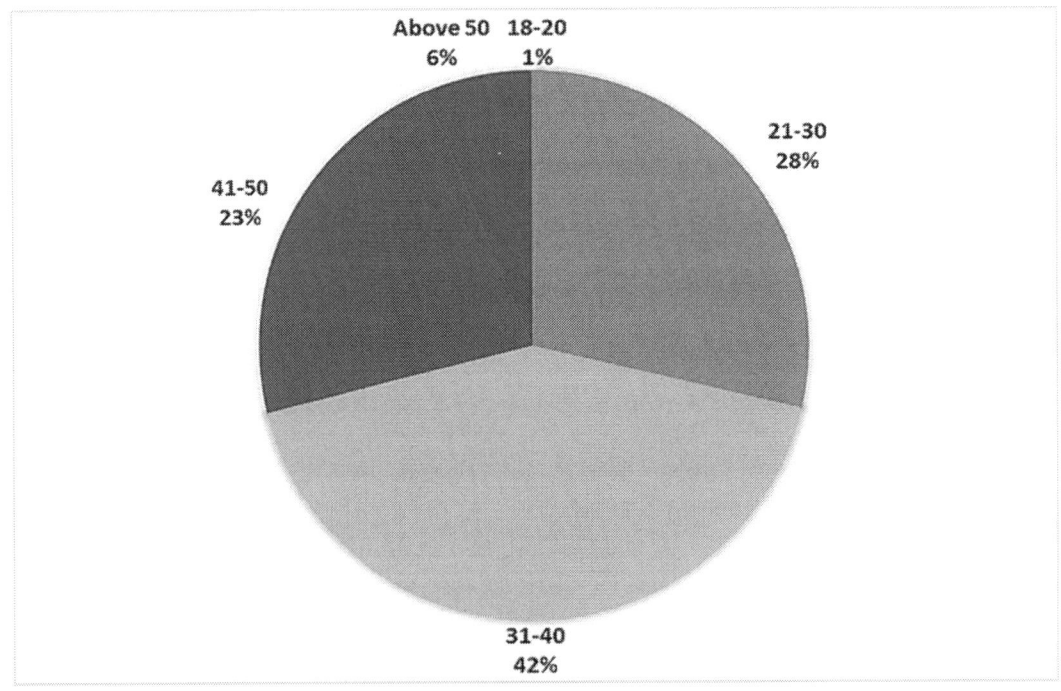

TABLE 3 - CONSTRUCT MEASURES AND DESCRIPTIVE STATISTICS

Scale Item	Variable Code	Mean	Standard Deviation
Interactivity			
My bank's website has a section for Frequently Asked Questions (FAQs)	Intera1	3.22	1.28
My bank has site navigation tools on their website	Intera2	3.42	1.25
My bank's website has a search tool that enables me to locate items	Intera3	3.60	1.29
Engagement			
I write comments and messages on my bank's Facebook page	Enga1	2.40	1.22
I 'like' content posted on my bank's Facebook page	Enga2	2.50	1.36
I retweet comments posted on my bank's Twitter handle	Enga3	2.10	1.26

Chapter Summary

Readers in this chapter, were taught about the various types of descriptive statistics, including frequencies, measures of central tendency and measures of dispersion. They learned how they can be used to describe and compare the basic characteristics of a sample and data set. Also, apart from learning how to derive descriptive statistics using SPSS software, they were also guided on how to present and interpret the output. Next, Chapter 5, will teach readers about the rubrics of Exploratory Factor Analysis (EFA).

Chapter 5

Exploratory Factor Analysis (EFA)

OBJECTIVES

In this chapter, Exploratory Factor Analysis (EFA) is dissected with a thorough discussion on what it is, the various forms of it and the steps involved in running an EFA in SPSS. This culminates in a discussion on the specific analysis output required, as well as how to present and interpret the resulting output.

What is Exploratory Factor Analysis (EFA)?

Exploratory Factor Analysis (EFA) is a statistical data reduction technique that is used to understand the relationships between variables by understanding the constructs that underlie them. The basic assumption of factor analysis is that for a set of observed (measured) variables there are a set of underlying variables called **factors** (unobserved or latent variables) that can explain the interrelationships among those variables. As such, researchers need to take cognizance of these two types of variables and what they mean when it comes to EFA; namely:

1. **Unobserved (Latent) Variables** - These are variables that are not directly observed but are deduced from other variables that are observed and directly measured. In a practical sense, latent variables are the constructs in the research framework for which researchers develop individual measurement items or statements for the purposes of data collection through questionnaires. For instance, Table 3 shows two latent variables, Interactivity and Engagement, with the individual observed variables (measurement items) that represent them.

2. **Observed (Measured) Variables** - These are variables that can be observed and directly measured. Practically observed variables are the individual statements or measurement items used in questionnaires for the purposes of data collection on specific research constructs. For instance, Table 3 shows all the individual observed variables (measurement items) that represent the constructs of Interactivity and Engagement.

Furthermore, EFA considers that any particular observed or measured variable can be linked with any of the factors presented in the research framework for which the data has been gathered.[34] Thus, EFA tries to mathematically derive an optimal number of factors to use in conveying as much of the information in the observed variables as possible. It is therefore an important tool for determining the number of latent variables within a set of observed variables.

THE 5-STEP EXPLORATORY FACTOR ANALYSIS PROTOCOL

There are five major steps a researcher must go through, to successfully perform an EFA and obtain an optimal set of factors that can be subsequently used in performing other higher order forms of quantitative analysis, like Multiple Regression and Structural Equation Modelling (SEM). These steps are presented in Figure 4.

FIGURE 4 - EFA PROTOCOL

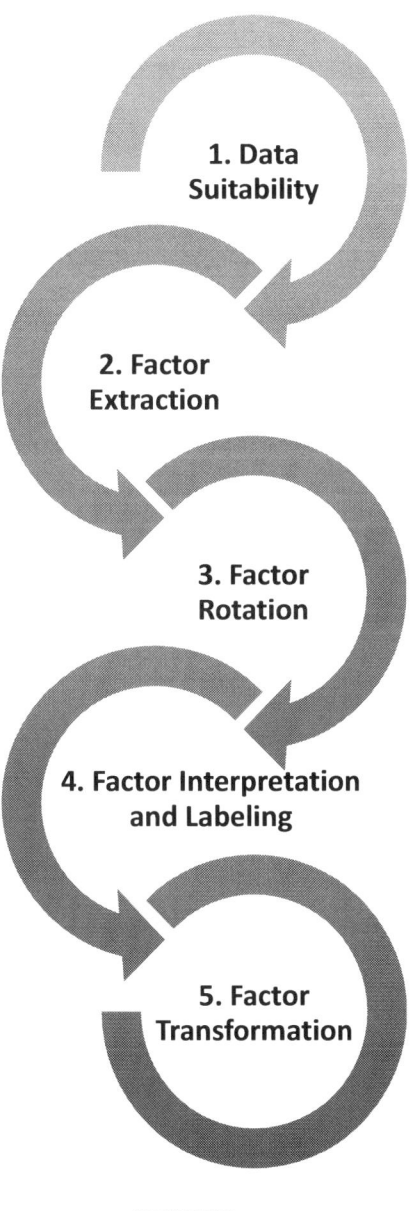

Data Suitability

Before a researcher can run an EFA, the suitability of the data set for EFA must be ascertained. The researcher must first of all ensure that there is some relationship between the variables, which can be determined by running a correlation analysis on the variables in the data set using SPSS. Tabachnick and Fidell[35] recommended inspecting the **correlation matrix** (which is generated as part of the SPSS output) for correlation coefficients over 0.30. While, Hair et al.[37] categorised these loadings using the following rule of thumb as ± 0.30 = minimal, ± 0.40 = important and ± 0.50 = practically significant. Although some level of correlation is desired between variables, high levels of correlation above 0.5 are not desirable. There should be some relationship between the variables, but, the relationship should not be very highly correlated with each other, as this can lead to multicollinearity issues.[35]

Also, the researcher must make sure he or she has a large enough sample size. There are several perspectives presented in the literature regarding what constitutes an adequate sample size. General guides include, Tabachnick's rule of thumb[35], which suggests having at least 300 cases for a data set to be suitable for factor analysis. Hair et al.[37] suggested that sample sizes should be 100 or greater. Others also cite the work of Comrey[38] in his guide to sample sizes: 100 being poor, 200 being fair, 300 being good, 500 as very good and 1000 or more as excellent. Using these guidelines, a researcher can appropriately determine the optimal sample size for their study or alternatively apply one of the sample size formulae discussed in Chapter 3 above to determine the best sample size to use, taking into consideration the objectives of their study.

Furthermore, SPSS generates other criteria as part of the EFA output to guide researchers in assessing the factorability of a given set of data. These include the **Kaiser-Meyer-Olkin (KMO) Measure of Sampling Adequacy**[39] and **Bartlett's Test of Sphericity**.[40] The KMO index indicates that there are sufficient items for each factor in the data set, whereas Bartlett's test of sphericity measures the overall significance of all correlations between the variables within a correlation matrix. The recommended threshold for the KMO index ranges from 0 to 1, with **0.60 and above** considered suitable for factor analysis.[37] KMO values that fall below **0.6** are not acceptable. They are an indication of an EFA that was conducted using an inadequate data set. While the Bartlett's Test of Sphericity should always be significant at **p ≤ 0.05** for the data set to be considered suitable for factor analysis. These are depicted in the subsequent practical demonstration of EFA in SPSS.

Factor Extraction

Factor extraction involves the researcher making a decision about how to go about extracting the optimal number of factors, as well as choosing the exact number of factors to extract.[36] There are several methods by which a researcher can extract factors from a data set. These include Principal Component Analysis (PCA), Principal Axis Factoring and Maximum Likelihood as provided in SPSS. Among these PCA is the one most often used for EFA, especially in published literature, since it enables the researcher to derive the minimum number of factors that explain the maximum amount of variance. PCA is also recommended when no prior theory or model exists.

Once the decision on how to extract the underlying factors in the data set has been made, the researcher must then determine the optimal number of factors to include for further analysis that he/she considers to best describe the underlying relationship among the variables that are of interest. Generally, theory is the primary means by which researchers can determine the number of underlying factors in a given data set. This is the only way that they can ascertain that the factors that have been extracted empirically exist. Nonetheless, there are other ways by which the researcher can identify the actual number of underlying factors in a particular data set. This is corroborated by existing literature, which recommends that multiple approaches be used in factor extraction. The most common approach to deciding this is by using **Kaiser's Criterion**, the **Cumulative percentage of variance** and the **Scree test**, as explained overleaf.

1. Kaiser's Criterion

Using this rule, only factors with an **eigenvalue of 1.0 or more** are retained for further investigation.[37] The eigenvalue of a factor represents the amount of the total variance explained by that principal component (factor). They can be either positive or negative in theory, but in practice they explain variance which is always positive. Therefore, researchers must note that if the eigenvalue of a component is negative it implies that the model is flawed, since variance cannot be negative.

2. Cumulative Percentage of Variance

The cumulative percentage of variance shown in the Total Variance Explained table (see SPSS output required) gives the percentage of variance accounted for by the first number of components with **eigenvalues > 1**. Although no fixed threshold exists, Hair et al.[37] proposes some for certain disciplines. For instance, in the natural sciences, they propose that factors should be stopped when at least 95% of the variance is explained. Whereas, for the humanities, they purport that the explained variance should usually be 50% or more. Although lower values are sometimes acceptable.

3. Scree test

The scree test involves plotting each of the eigenvalues of the factors on a graph and inspecting the plot to find a point at which the shape of the curve changes; the elbow, or break in the plot, as these factors contribute the most to the explanation of the variance in the data set. Tabachnick and Fidell[35] note that interpreting scree plots is relatively subjective, relying mainly on researcher judgment.

Alternatively, the researcher can carry out a forced factor extraction using SPSS Statistics. This simply involves a number of additional steps where you instruct SPSS Statistics to retain a specific number of components instead of basing it on eigenvalues greater than 1. This will provide a relatively different outcome.

Factor Rotation

Factor rotation comes after the factors have been extracted, with the aim of achieving a simpler and more meaningful factor solution. It was observed earlier in this chapter that any particular observed variable can be linked with any of the factors represented in the data set. As a result, the researcher must make sure that each variable relates to one and only one factor. This makes the outcome easier to interpret. To achieve this aim, the factors are "rotated". Rotation maximizes high item loadings and minimizes low item loadings, therefore producing a more interpretable and simplified solution. Note that this does not change the underlying EFA solution; it merely presents the pattern of factor loadings in a manner that is easier to interpret; with each variable loading highly on one and only one component. **Factor loadings** (factor or component coefficients) as used here refer to the correlation coefficients between the observed variables and the factors that they measure. It shows the strength of the association of each observed variable with their underlying factor. Variables with high loadings are usually preferred, particularly those with loadings of **0.5 and above**.[35]

There are two main approaches to factor rotation, resulting in either an orthogonal (uncorrelated factors) or oblique (correlated factors) factor solutions:

1. **Orthogonal rotation technique** - This approach to rotation assumes that each factor is independent of or orthogonal to all other factors. Thus, it produces factor structures that are uncorrelated. Examples of this technique are Varimax, Quartimax and Equamax rotation. But, Varimax is the most popular among these.

2. **Oblique rotation technique** - This approach to rotation identifies the extent to which each of the factors are correlated with each other. Thus, it produces factor structures that are

correlated. Examples of this technique are Direct Oblimin and Promax rotation, with Promax being the more popular of the two.

SPSS provides the various rotation techniques within each of the two rotational approaches, as shown in the practical demonstration of EFA below.

Factor Interpretation and Labeling

Factor interpretation involves the researcher examining which variables or measurement items are attributable to a given factor and giving that factor a name or label based on the prevailing theme among the variables. Generally, each factor must have at least two or three variables loading on it, to facilitate a meaningful interpretation. For instance, a factor may include a set of four variables which all relate to the quality of services offered; therefore, the researcher would create a label of **"service quality"** for that factor. The interpretation and labeling of factors is a highly subjective, theoretical, and inductive process. It relies heavily on the researcher's judgment[41], as well as empirical research in the specific area of study. Nevertheless, it is imperative that the resulting factor labels reflect the researcher's theoretical and conceptual intent.

Factor Transformation

Factor transformation enables the researcher to condense several variables that measure the same factor into one. It involves the researcher computing the individual variables that load together, into single variables to form the factors that they represent. This is useful for running inferential statistics like Simple Linear and Multiple Regression analysis.

The manner in which researchers can proceed through each of these five stages in SPSS is practically demonstrated in the next section.

Practical Demonstration of Exploratory Factor Analysis (EFA) - PCA

A researcher run a survey among 600 retail bank customers in order to determine if their loyalty to their primary bank was influenced by their level of engagement and personalized interactions with their bank online (i.e., these are the three main constructs we are interested in). The questions in the survey were phrased such that customers' loyalty was captured by **BehLo 1-7**, the level of engagement with their bank online was captured as **Eng 1-7** and the questions coded as **Pers 1-8** represented the personalized interactions between the bank and their customers online. The procedure for running the EFA on the resulting data set is presented below.

Procedure in SPSS

1. Click **Analyze** > **Dimension Reduction** > **Factor** on the top menu, as shown below:

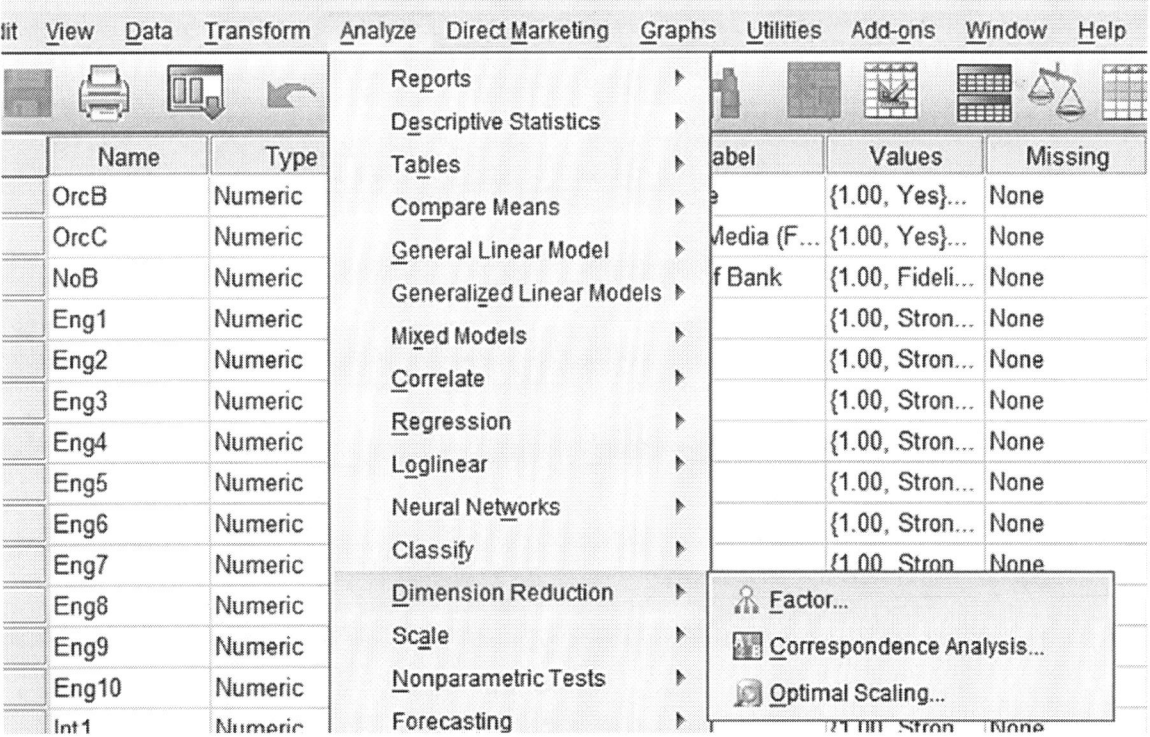

2. You will be presented with the **Factor Analysis** dialogue box, as shown below:

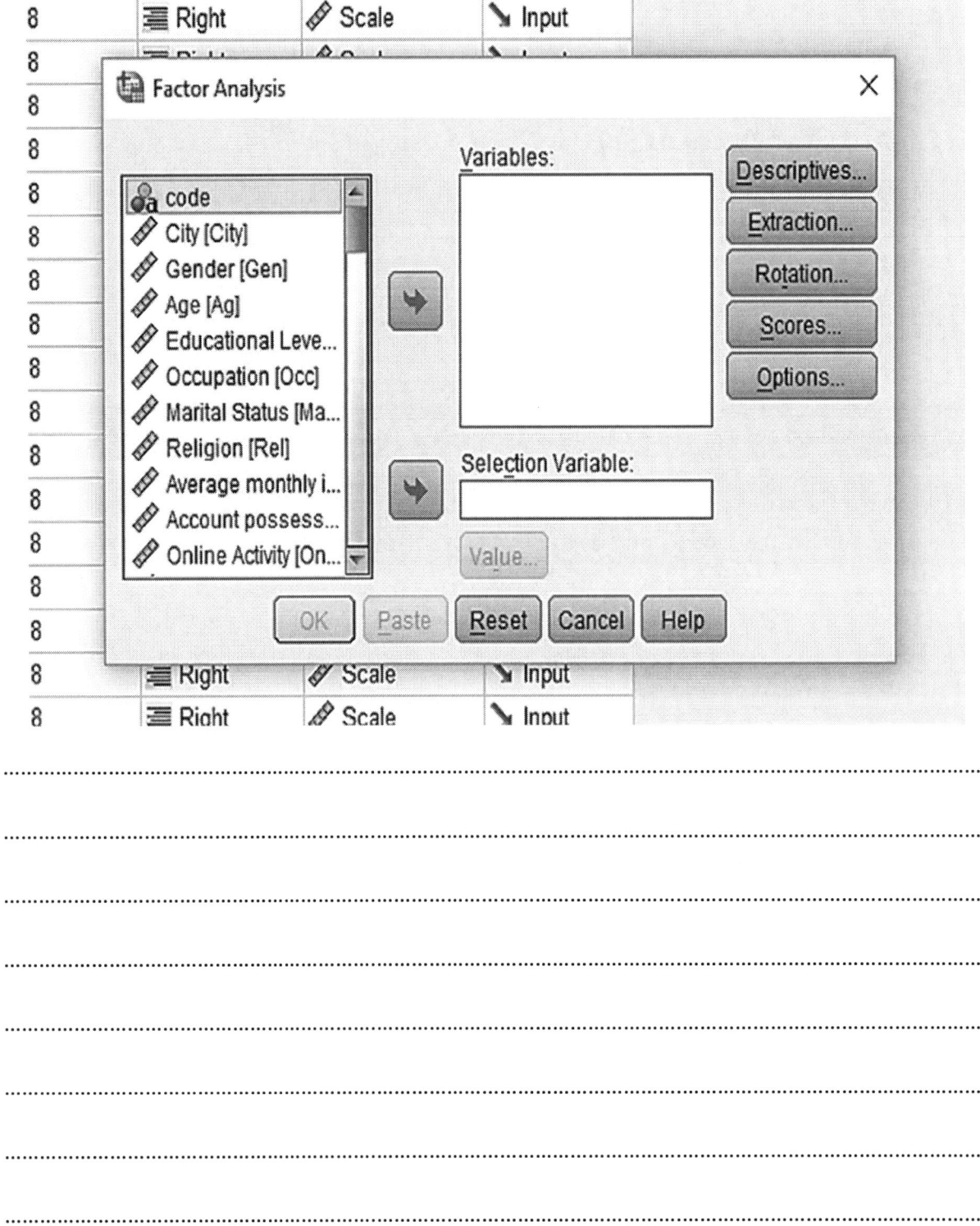

3. Transfer the variables that you want to be included in the factor analysis into the **Variable(s)** box by either dragging-and-dropping or using the arrow button, as seen below. In this example, we transfer the variables **BehLo 1-7**, **Eng 1-7** and **Pers 1-8.**

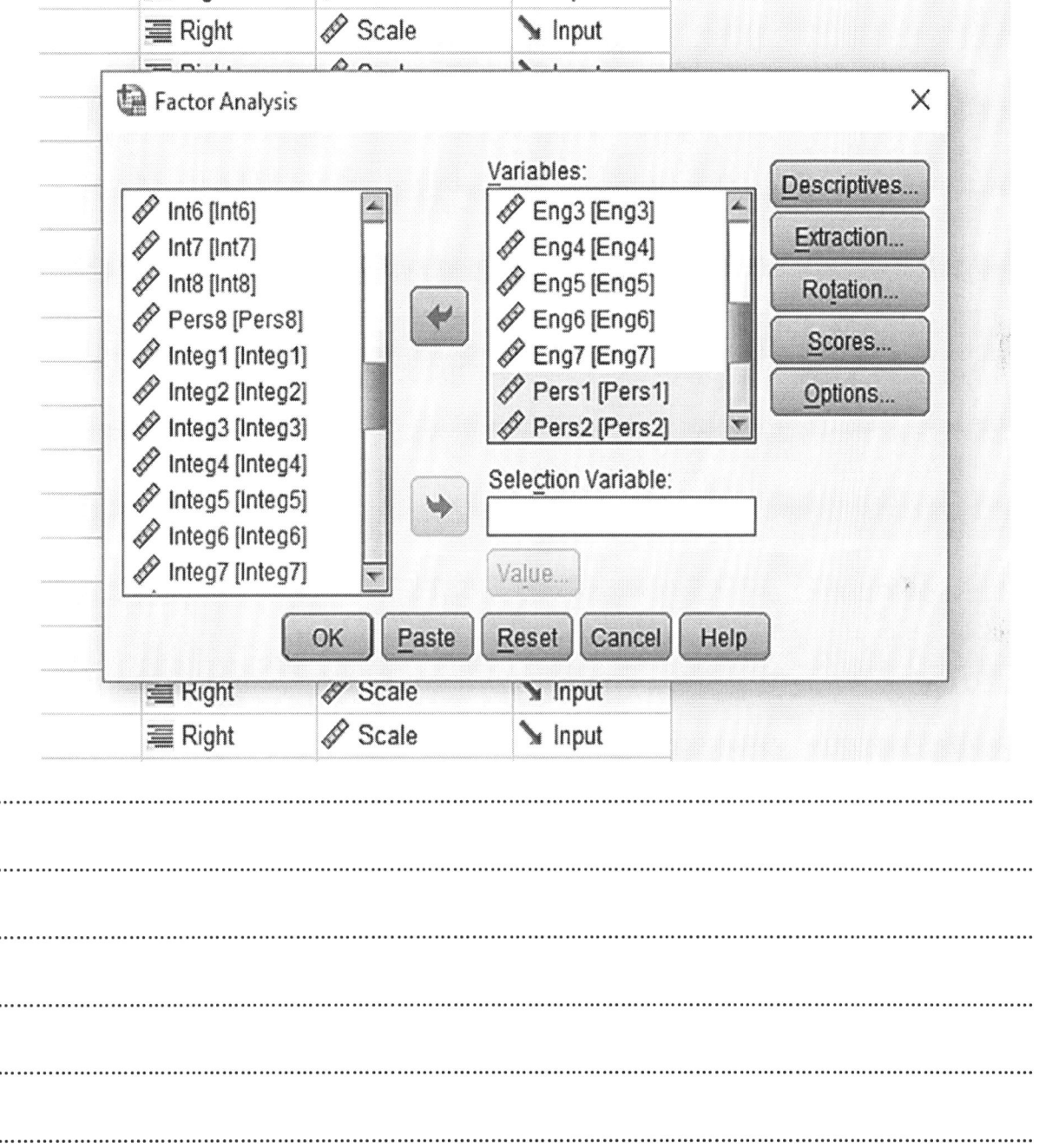

4. Click the **Descriptives** button. You will be presented with the **Factor Analysis: Descriptives** dialogue box, as shown below.

   ❖ Leave **Initial solution** checked in the *Statistics* area.
   ❖ Select **Coefficients**, **Significance levels**, **KMO and Bartlett's test of sphericity**, **Reproduced** and **Anti-image** in the *Correlation Matrix* area.

   You will end up with a screen similar to the one below.

   ❖ Click **Continue**.

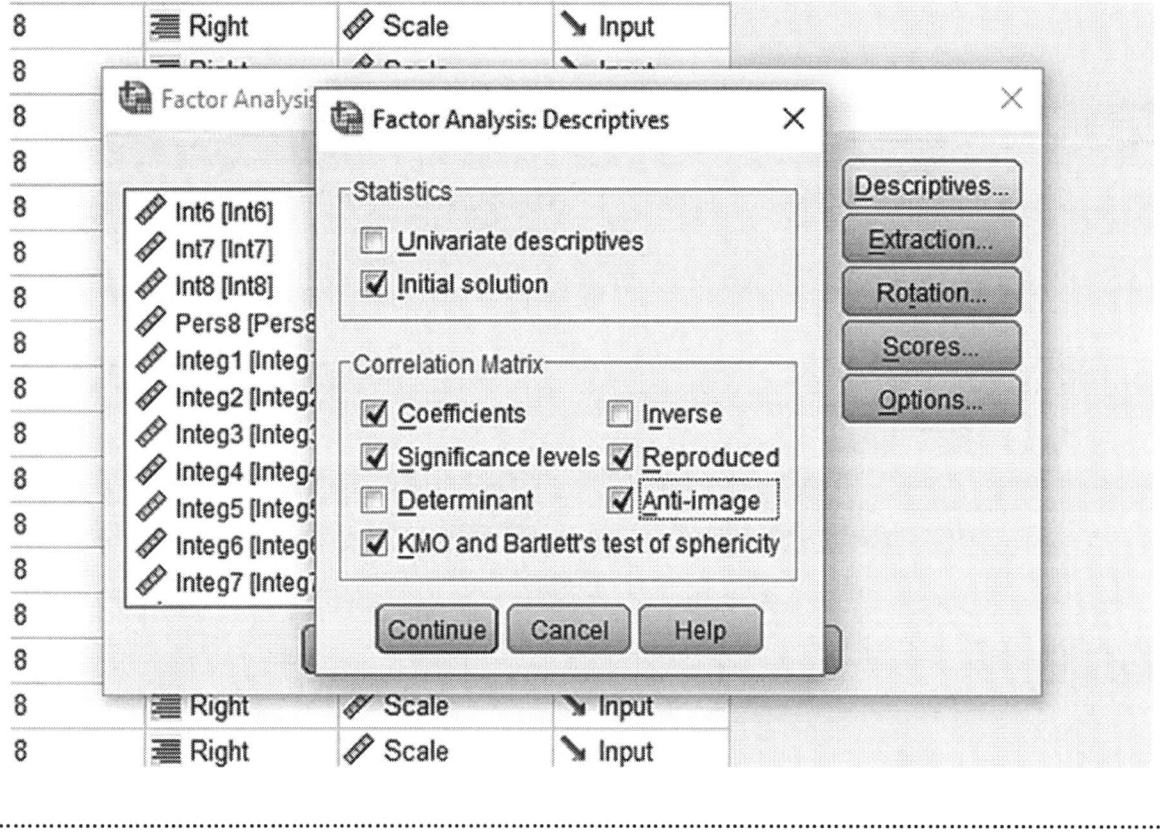

5. Click the **Extraction** button. You will be presented with the **Factor Analysis: Extraction** dialogue box, as shown below.

   ❖ Select **Principal components** in the *Method* area.
   ❖ Leave **Correlation matrix** checked in the *Analyze* area.
   ❖ Leave **Unrotated factor solution** checked in the *Display* area.
   ❖ In the **Extract** area, either select **Based on Eigenvalue** and set **Eigenvalues greater than:** to **1**; or set a **Fixed number of factors** to extract
   ❖ **Maximum iterations for convergence** should be set to **25**.

You will end up with a screen like the one below.

   ❖ Click **Continue**.

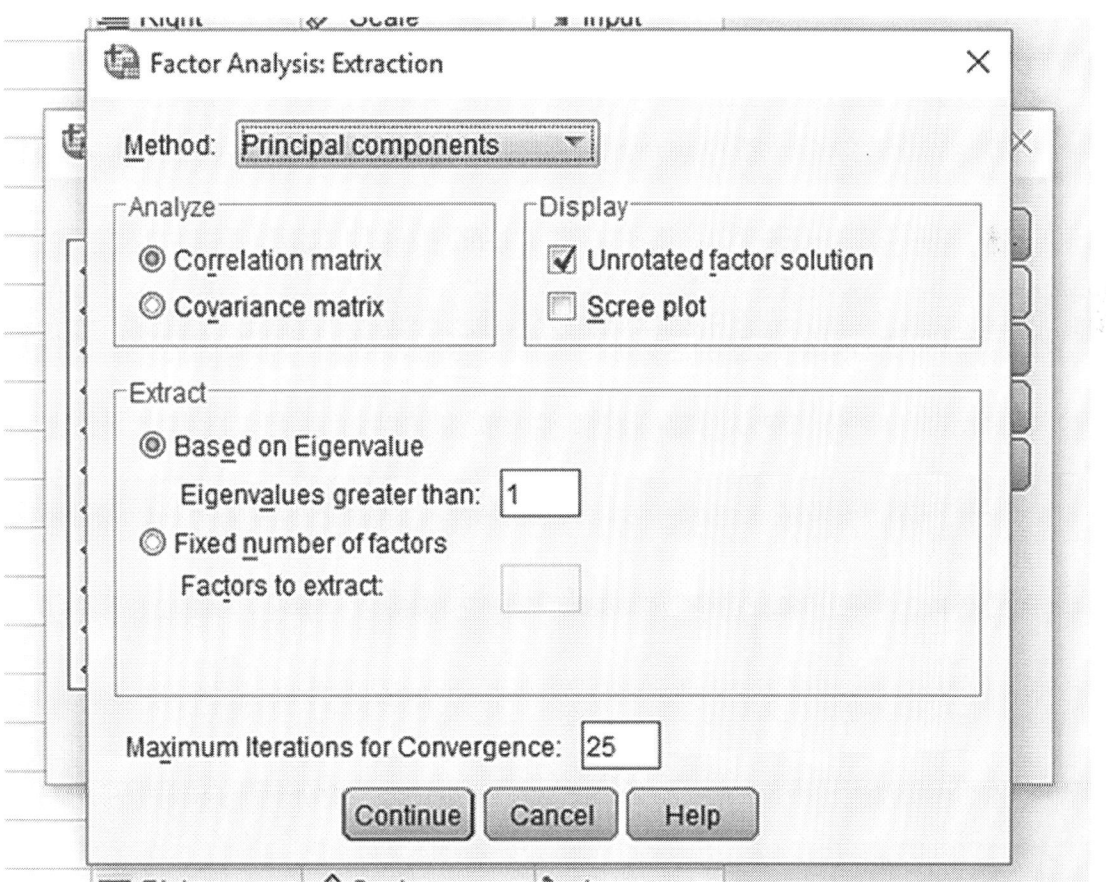

6. Click the **Rotation** button. You will be presented with the **Factor Analysis: Rotation** dialogue box, as shown below.

   ❖ Select **Varimax** in the *Method* area.
   ❖ Leave **Rotated solution** checked in the *Display* area.
   ❖ **Maximum iterations for convergence** should be set to **25**, as seen below.
   ❖ Click **Continue**.

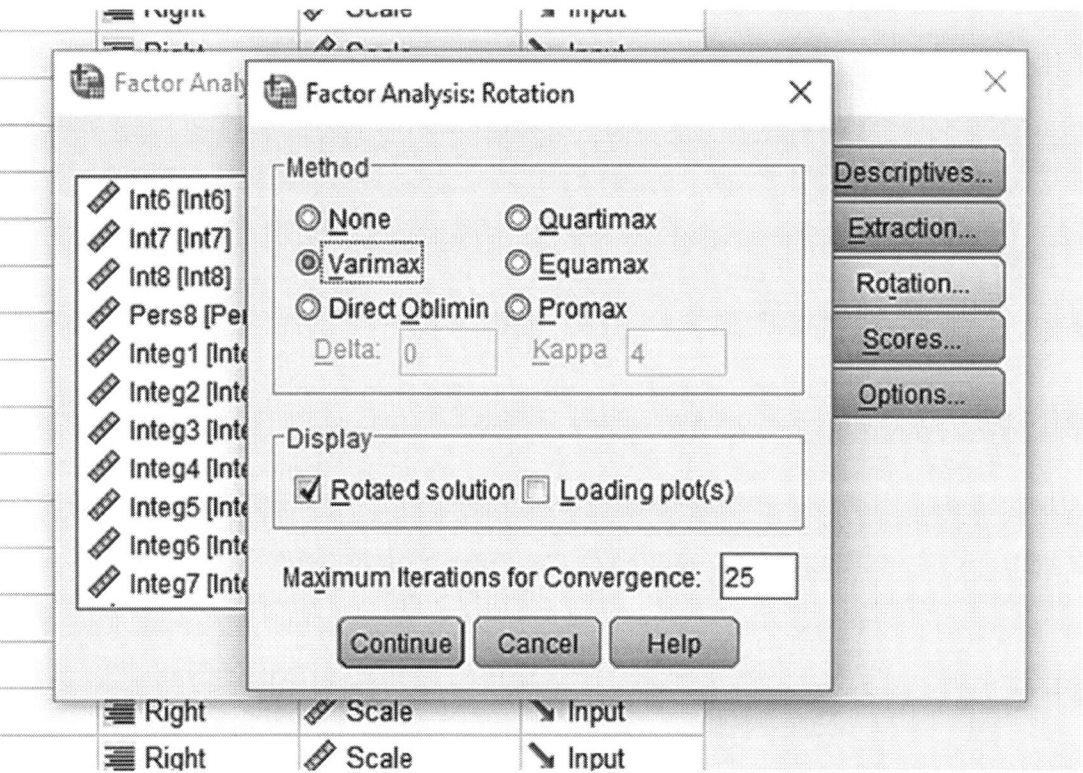

7. Click the **Options** button. You will be presented with the **Factor Analysis: Options** dialogue box, as shown below.

   ❖ Leave **Exclude cases listwise** checked in the *Missing Values* area.
   ❖ Select **Suppress small coefficients.**
   ❖ Change the **Absolute value** below from **0.1** to **0.5** in the *Coefficient Display Format* area.

   You will end up with a screen like the one below.

   ❖ Click **Continue**.

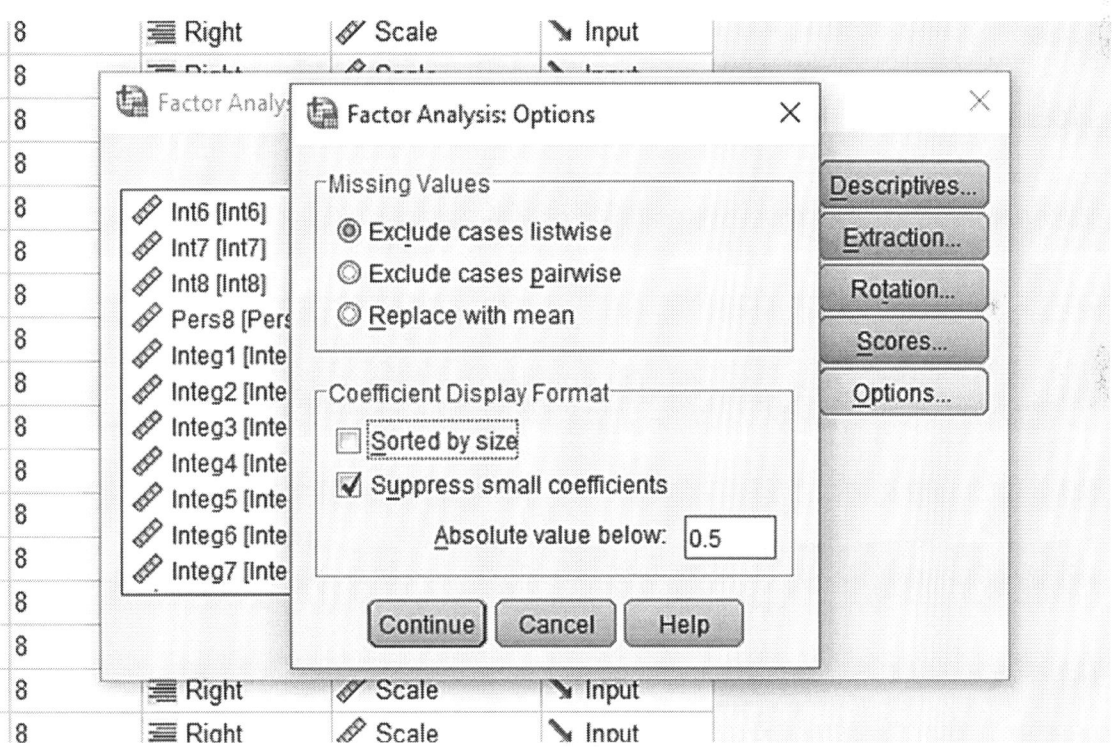

8. Click the **Continue** button and then click **OK** to generate the output.

SPSS Output Required

The output generated by SPSS is rather extensive and can provide a lot of information on your analysis. However, the main output required is that of the **KMO and Bartlett's Test**, **Total Variance Explained** and **Rotated Component Matrix**, as observed below.

KMO and Bartlett's Test		
Kaiser-Meyer-Olkin Measure of Sampling Adequacy.		.918
Bartlett's Test of Sphericity	Approx. Chi-Square	8879.065
	df	210
	Sig.	.000

Total Variance Explained

Component	Initial Eigenvalues			Extraction Sums of Squared Loadings			Rotation Sums of Squared Loadings		
	Total	% of Variance	Cumulative %	Total	% of Variance	Cumulative %	Total	% of Variance	Cumulative %
1	8.378	39.895	39.895	8.378	39.895	39.895	7.054	33.590	33.590
2	2.531	12.054	51.949	2.531	12.054	51.949	2.372	11.293	44.883
3	1.378	6.563	58.512	1.378	6.563	58.512	2.187	10.412	55.295
4	1.267	6.034	64.545	1.267	6.034	64.545	1.943	9.250	64.545
5	.998	4.750	69.296						
6	.901	4.293	73.588						
7	.824	3.923	77.511						
8	.758	3.610	81.121						
9	.649	3.088	84.209						
10	.576	2.745	86.954						
11	.442	2.104	89.058						
12	.408	1.941	90.999						
13	.370	1.762	92.761						
14	.364	1.735	94.496						
15	.287	1.367	95.863						
16	.219	1.044	96.906						
17	.183	.872	97.778						
18	.166	.789	98.567						
19	.150	.716	99.283						
20	.087	.413	99.696						
21	.064	.304	100.000						

Extraction Method: Principal Component Analysis.

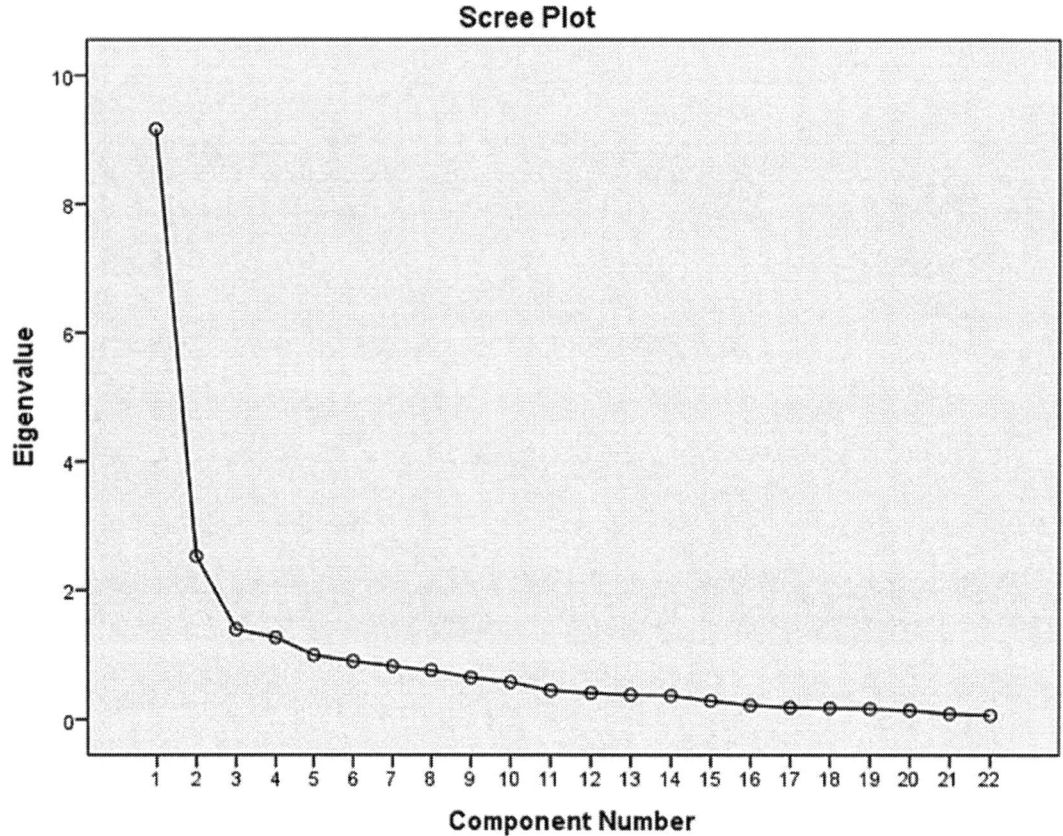

Rotated Component Matrix[a]				
	Component			
	1	2	3	4
BehLo1			.655	
BehLo2				
BehLo3				.564
BehLo4				.651
BehLo5				.581
BehLo6				.574
BehLo7				
Eng1	.873			
Eng2		.858		
Eng3		.864		
Eng4	.816			
Eng5	.891			
Eng6	.917			
Eng7	.814			
Pers1			.820	
Pers2			.756	
Pers3	.676			
Pers4	.901			
Pers5	.884			
Pers6	.829			
Pers7		.694		

Extraction Method: Principal Component Analysis.
Rotation Method: Varimax with Kaiser Normalization.
a. Rotation converged in 7 iterations.

It can be inferred from the discussion above that the exploratory factor analysis may have to be re-run a number of times before arriving at a final factor solution for the data set. However, once the researcher arrives at a final solution, having successfully delineated the different sets of variables that represent each of the factors extracted, they can then proceed to transform the variables into unique individual factors. The steps for achieving this are presented overleaf.

Factor Transformation

1. Click **Transform** > **Compute variable** as shown below:

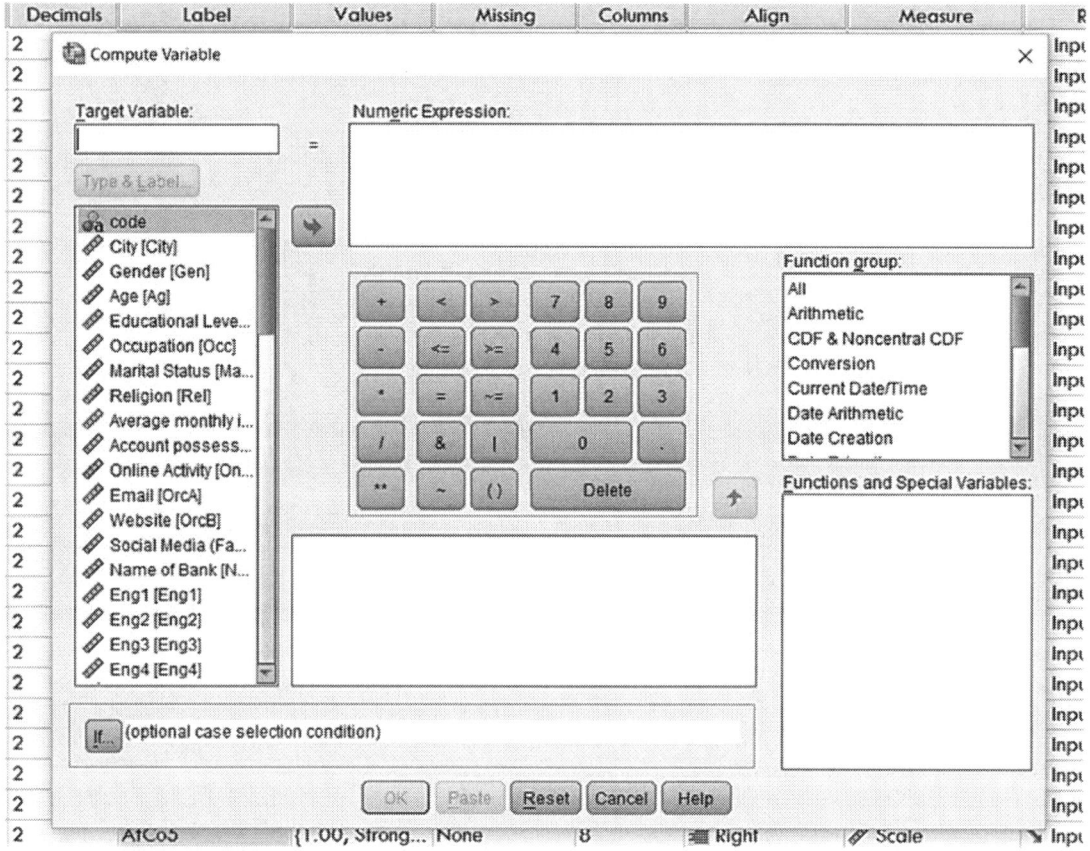

2. In the **Target Variable** box, type a name for the new variable that will be computed. Let's call our new variable for Factor 4 "**BehaviouralLoyalty**". This will be made up of **BehLo3**, **BehLo4**, **BehLo5** and **BehLo6** per the rotated component matrix above. Kindly note that in creating a name for the new variable you cannot use special characters such as **&**, -, * or even a space between words. These are all considered illegal characters by SPSS. The underscore (_) is however, allowed.

In the **Numeric Expression** box, add up all the individual variables that make up the factor, per the rotated component matrix and compute their average. This is done by moving the variables in question from the left column to the Numeric Expression box and then writing the expression around them. This expression indicates that the new variable, **BehaviouralLoyalty,** will be calculated as **BehLo3** + **BehLo4** + **BehLo5** + **BehLo6**, divided by **4**, as seen in the image below.

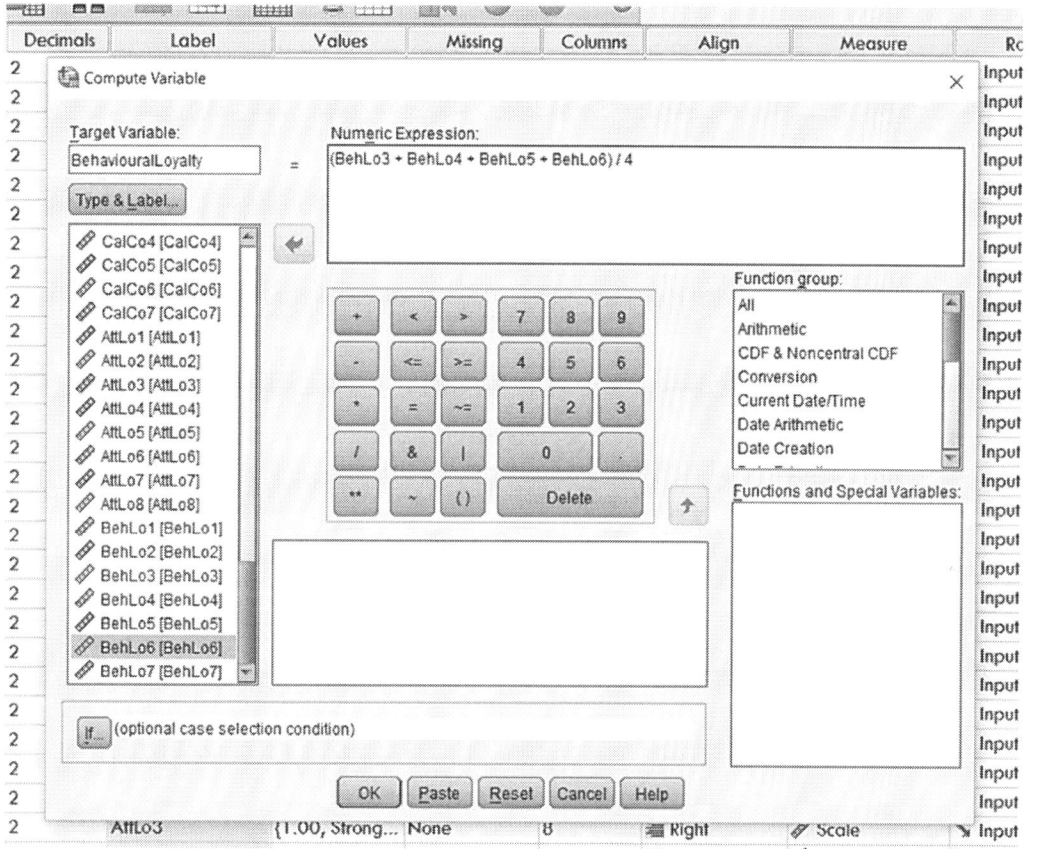

3. Click **OK** to complete the computation and generate the output.

The new variable that has been created can be viewed in the last column in the **Data View** window or in the last row of the **Variable View** window of the SPSS file. If you do not see the new variable, the computation was unsuccessful. The researcher can then go ahead and reset the **Compute Variable** window and redo it or otherwise compute for the remaining factors (components) identified.

Analyzing Exploratory Factor Analysis (EFA) Output

Explanations of the key analysis output that is required in order to adequately interpret the EFA results are provided below.

1. First, the results from the data suitability tests need to be interpreted to make sure that you can use EFA to analyze your data. This mainly includes examining:

   a) The **Kaiser-Meyer-Olkin (KMO) Measure of Sampling Adequacy** for the overall data set. This value must be 0.6 and above in order to make factor analysis appropriate.[37]

   b) The **Bartlett's test of sphericity** to ascertain if the data is suitable for reduction. This test must be significant ($p \leq 0.05$) for factor analysis to be appropriate.

2. Second, the factor extraction results must be interpreted. An inspection of **the Total Variance Explained** table must be conducted with a focus on the **Total** column under the **Initial Eigen values** section to identify the number of components (factors) to be extracted. Using Kaiser's criterion and the Scree plot, (as explained earlier), we are interested only in components that have an eigenvalue of 1 or more. In the example above, only the first four components recorded eigenvalues above 1 (8.38, 2.53, 1.38, 1.27). These four components explain a total of 64.55% of the variance as shown in the **Cumulative %** column under the **Extraction Sums of Squared Loadings section**.

3. Third is the factor rotation results that will lead to each variable loading highly on one factor. This will give a clear set of variables that relate to each factor. The goal is to achieve a simple structure where you have a readily explainable division of variables onto separate components, with at least three variables loading onto each component. In this example, orthogonal rotation (varimax) is used; meaning that the final factors will be as uncorrelated as possible with each other. Hence, we can assume that the information explained by one factor is independent of the information in the other factors.

EXPLORATORY FACTOR ANALYSIS (EFA) FOR SEM

In conducting EFA for the purposes of Structural Equation Modelling (SEM), the procedure is slightly different than if the EFA was conducted, for instance, for a Multiple Regression analysis. In running a SEM analysis, it is necessary, though not compulsory, that researchers employ EFA first prior to moving on to the process of Confirmatory Factor Analysis (CFA). Generally, EFA is used to separate the unique and uncorrelated measurement items from the correlated ones in the data set. This makes the resulting model easier to validate using CFA. Thus, to perform EFA with the intention of validating the resulting model using CFA, for the purpose of Structural Equation Modelling, the procedure is as follows.

Procedure in SPSS

1. Click **Analyze** > **Dimension Reduction** > **Factor** on the top menu, as shown below:

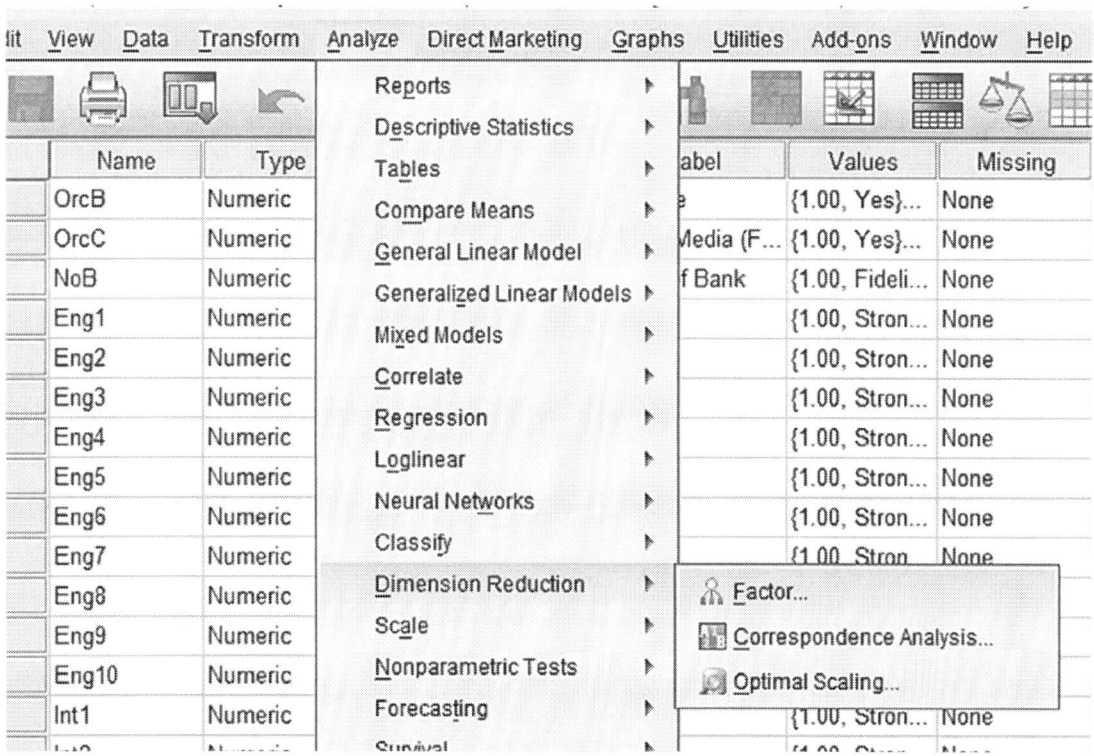

2. You will be presented with the **Factor Analysis** dialogue box, as shown below:

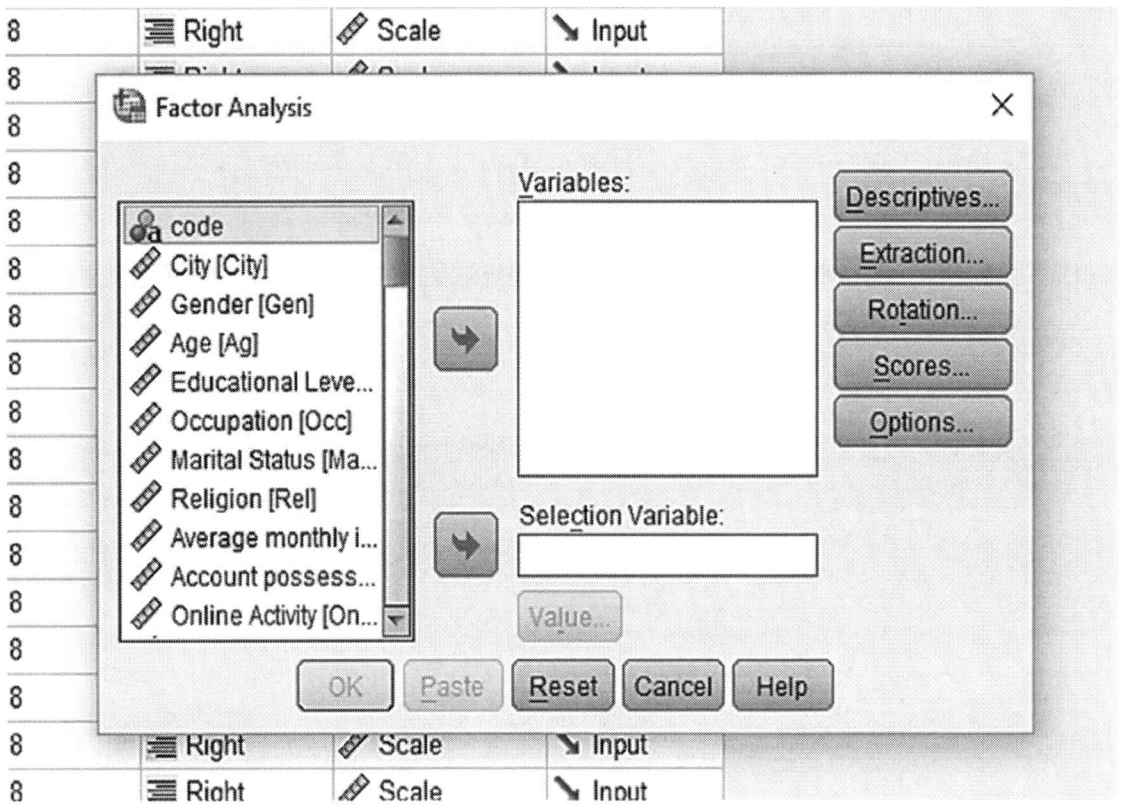

3. Transfer the variables that you want to be included in the factor analysis into the **Variable(s)** box by either dragging-and-dropping or using the arrow button, as seen below. In this example, we transfer the variables **BehLo 1-7**, **Eng 1-7** and **Pers 1-8**.

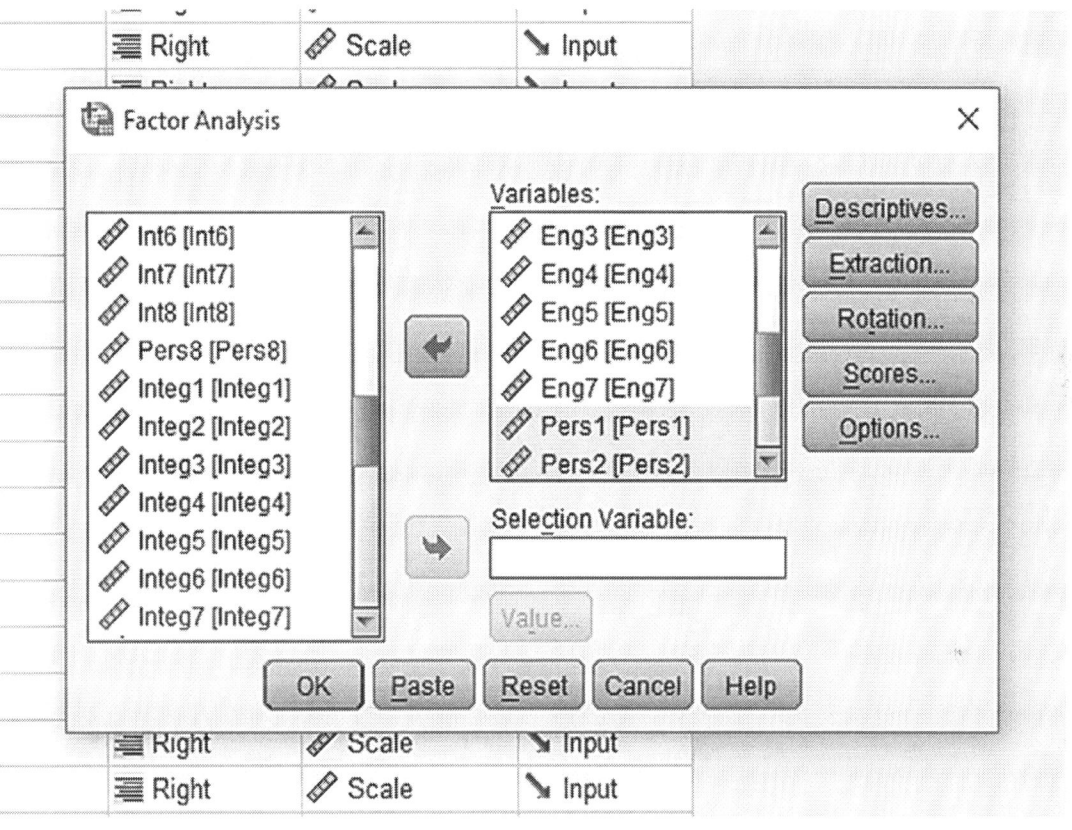

4. Click the **Descriptives** button. You will be presented with the **Factor Analysis: Descriptives** dialogue box, as shown below.

   ❖ Leave **Initial solution** checked in the *Statistics* area.
   ❖ Select **Coefficients**, **Significance levels**, **KMO and Bartlett's test of sphericity**, **Reproduced** and **Anti-image** in the *Correlation Matrix* area.

   You will end up with a screen similar to the one below.

   ❖ Click **Continue**.

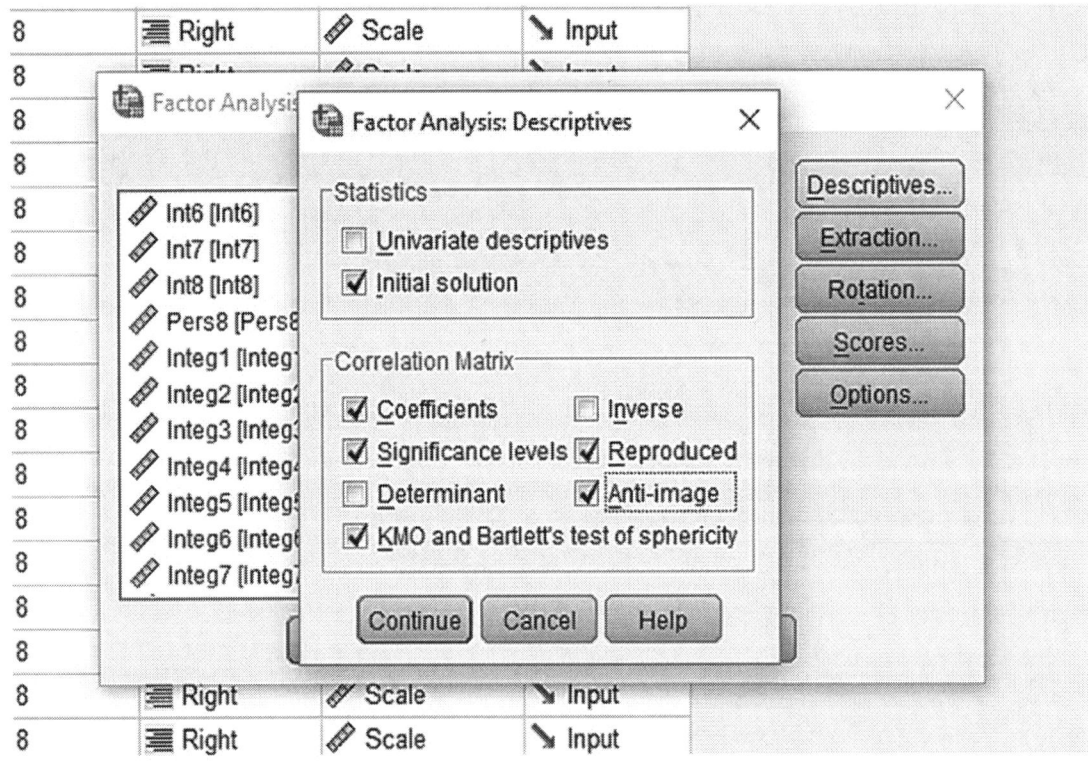

5. Click the **Extraction** button. You will be presented with the **Factor Analysis: Extraction** dialogue box, as shown below.

   ❖ Select **Maximum Likelihood** in the *Method* area.
   ❖ Leave **Unrotated factor solution** checked in the *Display* area.
   ❖ In the **Extract** area, either select **Based on Eigenvalue** and set **Eigenvalues greater than:** to **1**; or set a **Fixed number of factors** to extract
   ❖ **Maximum iterations for convergence** should be set to **25**.

   You will end up with a screen like the one below.

   ❖ Click **Continue**.

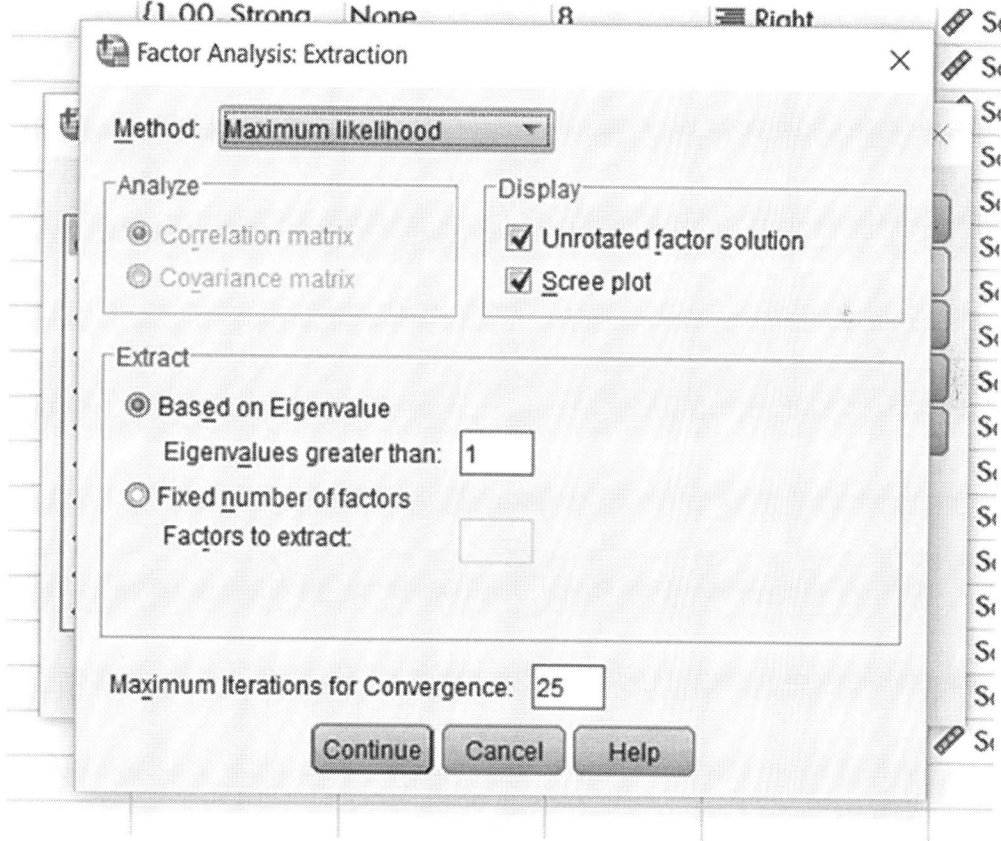

6. Click the **Rotation** button. You will be presented with the **Factor Analysis: Rotation** dialogue box, as shown below.
   - ❖ Select **Promax** in the *Method* area.
   - ❖ Leave **Rotated solution** checked in the *Display* area.
   - ❖ **Maximum iterations for convergence** should be set to **25**, as seen below.
   - ❖ Click **Continue**.

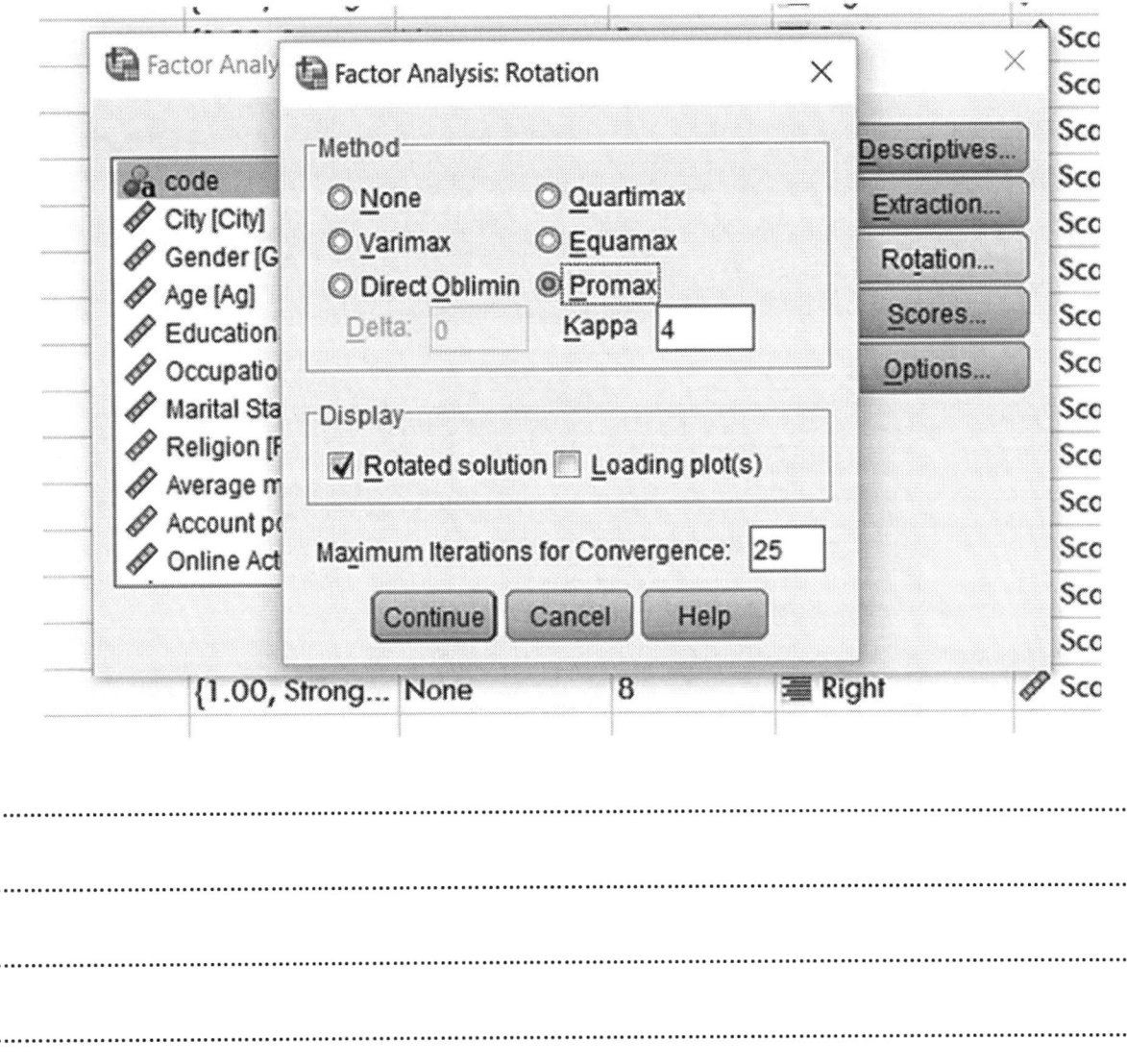

7. Click the **Options** button. You will be presented with the **Factor Analysis: Options** dialogue box, as shown below.

   ❖ Leave **Exclude cases listwise** checked in the *Missing Values* area.
   ❖ Select **Suppress small coefficients.**
   ❖ Change the **Absolute values** below from **0.1** to **0.5** in the *Coefficient Display Format* area.

   You will end up with a screen like the one below.

   ❖ Click **Continue**.

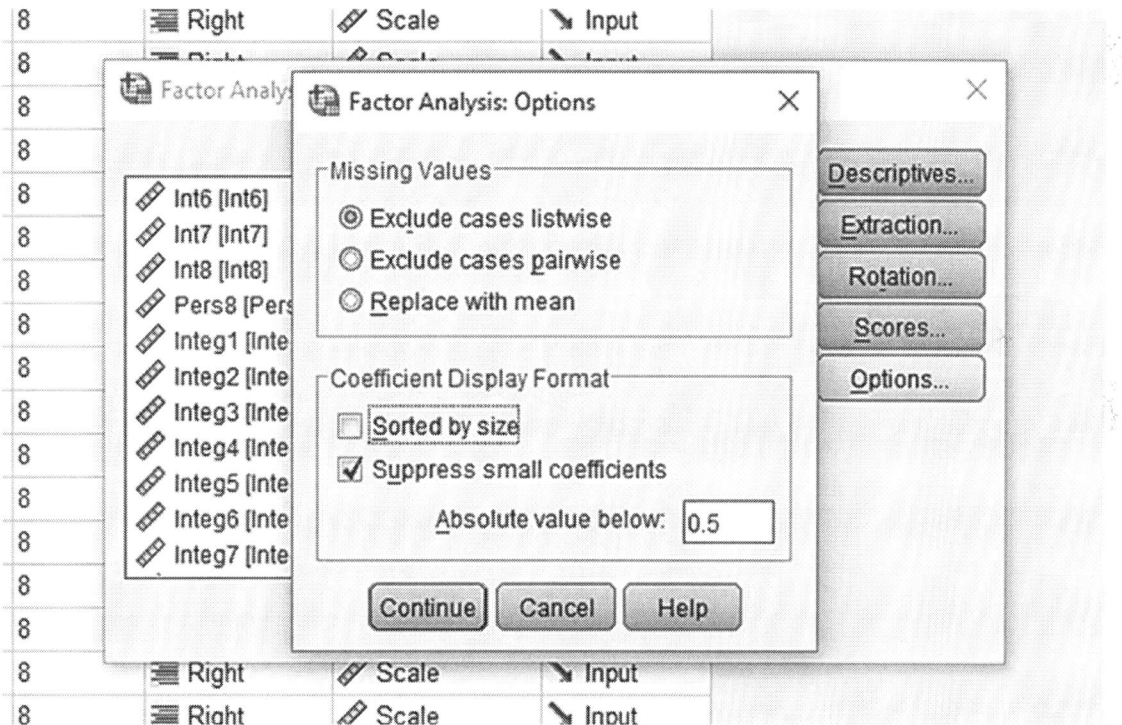

8. Click the **Continue** button and then click **OK** to generate the output.

Here we notice that the extraction method selected is the **Maximum Likelihood** method, in place of the previously selected Principal components. This is because the **Maximum Likelihood** approach allows for the computation of a wide range of indices on the goodness of fit of the model and permits statistical significance testing of factor loadings and correlations among factors, as well as the computation of confidence intervals; all of which are an integral part of SEM analysis.[43]

Furthermore, the factor rotation method selected here is an **Oblique rotation** technique, which identifies the extent to which each of the factors are correlated with each other. The **Promax** technique is particularly selected for SEM to enable the researcher to extract the optimal number of factors, at the same time considering the underlying intercorrelations between them.[42]

SPSS Output Required

Similarly, the output generated by SPSS using this method is rather extensive and can provide a lot of information on your analysis. However, the main output required apart from those stated above for SEM is the **Pattern Matrix**, as depicted overleaf. It shows the factor loadings of each of the individual variables with their respective factors. The **Pattern Matrix** is required to pair with the **Pattern Matrix Model Builder** in Amos (see Chapter 8), to construct a preliminary path diagram for further analysis using CFA.

Pattern Matrix[a]				
	Factor			
	1	2	3	4
Eng1	.869			
Eng2		.929		
Eng3		.970		
Eng4	.788			
Eng5	.941			
Eng6	.996			
Eng7	.787			
Pers1				.823
Pers2				.685
Pers3	.607			
Pers4	.928			
Pers5	.897			
Pers6	.829			
Pers7		.537		
BehLo1				
BehLo2				
BehLo3				
BehLo4				
BehLo5			.596	
BehLo6				
BehLo7				

Extraction Method: Maximum Likelihood.
Rotation Method: Promax with Kaiser Normalization.
a. Rotation converged in 5 iterations.

Chapter Summary

This chapter discussed Exploratory Factor Analysis (EFA), looking into the 5 step EFA protocol, as well as the various methods of conducting EFA depending on the purpose for which the output will be used, including the type of EFA required to enable a researcher to perform a Structural Equation Modelling (SEM) analysis. The output required from SPSS, as well as how to present and interpret this output was discussed. Now, Chapter 6 will discuss construct reliability and validity.

Chapter Review

Question 1

Identify a journal of your choice and compare and contrast the methodology and analysis sections of two published articles which used exploratory factor analysis.

Chapter 6

Reliability and Validity

OBJECTIVES

This chapter discusses how to assess a set of reliability and validity of the constructs used in a given research model. It discusses the important role of reliability and validity play in quantitative data analysis, as well as how to test for them. Readers are also taught about the different criteria required for a construct to satisfy the dimensions of reliability and validity. Furthermore, they learn how to compute these measures of reliability and validity using SPSS and Microsoft Excel software.

WHY RELIABILITY AND VALIDITY?

Social science researchers face unique difficulties when it comes to measuring constructs in their research. This is partly due to the fact that they are studying human behavior within various social structures. As a result, they often face the challenge of not knowing if the scales they develop are actually measuring what they set out to measure. Therefore, in order to address this issue, social science researchers go ahead to test these scales to ensure that:

1. **They measure the intended construct(s) consistently and precisely.**
2. **They indeed measure the latent construct that they wanted to measure.**

This is considered in statistical terms as testing for scale reliability and validity respectively. These are jointly called the ***psychometric properties*** of measurement scales and constitute the yardsticks against which the adequacy and accuracy of our measurement instruments are evaluated in quantitative scientific research.[51]

Reliability and validity are two distinct but closely related concepts in multivariate data analysis. They are related in the sense that although reliability is a necessary condition for validity, the existence of reliability is not a sufficient premise for the validity of an instrument.[44] Therefore, they must be treated as such. **Reliability** is the degree to which the data collection techniques and analysis procedures will yield consistent, reproducible findings.[45] It is directly linked with the level of error in the research findings, such that the larger the reliability value the less the amount of error. While, **Validity** captures the extent to which a measurement instrument actually measures what it is purported to measure. It stands for the truthfulness or correctness of a measurement instrument for a certain purpose and definition. This is because a measurement item may be a valid measure for a particular factor but be less valid or even invalid for another factor.

Though the boundary between the two concepts is often blurred, a measurement scale that is reliable may not necessarily be valid; they both vary individually.[45] Furthermore, literature observes that validity is relatively more difficult to achieve than reliability. Measures can sometimes be reliable but not valid, if they are measuring a construct consistently, but are consistently measuring the wrong construct. Similarly, measures can be valid but not reliable if they measure the right construct, but not consistently. Hence, the need to independently assess the reliability and the validity of the measurement instrument, as well as the measurement scales for each construct; especially in higher order analysis techniques like Structural Equation Modelling (SEM). Reliability and validity in SEM are usually assessed during Confirmatory Factor Analysis (CFA), as part of the estimation of the measurement model (see Chapter 8). Literature asserts that the reliability and validity of the scales used in quantitative data analysis must be assessed to ensure that the individual items which come together to form a factor are free from random error and all measure the same attribute.[46] Thereby, emphasizing the pertinence of reliability and validity tests in SEM.

Assessing Reliability

There are two main reliability criteria required, in order to effectively assess a measurement model in SEM. These are: **Internal consistency** and **Test-Retest reliability**, as explained below.

1. **Internal consistency -** This shows how much a set of items that propose to measure the same construct actually measure the construct in question.[45]

2. **Test-Retest reliability -** This shows the likelihood that the measurement scale for a given construct will consistently yield the same output when tested.[44]

Cronbach's Alpha (α) is the most commonly applied estimate of the internal consistency of a multiple-item scale.[47] Several authors suggest different levels of the Cronbach's Alpha (α) estimates, which satisfy the criteria for reliability.[33,45] Some researchers aver that if Cronbach's Alpha (α) is closer to 0 then the data is not reliable at all; whereas if it is closer to 1 then the data is very reliable. Others assert that coefficients that fall between **0.7** and **0.9** are acceptable[45], with **0.6** being the lower limit of acceptability.[33] But, despite being the most used reliability measure, Cronbach's Alpha (α) is not sufficient for assessing the overall reliability of a measurement instrument.

Research proffers that the Cronbach's Alpha (α) estimate is a function of the number of items in the scale.[48] Thus, if a scale has many items it can have high α values even though the average correlation among the individual items may be very small. Hence, through CFA, the **Composite Reliability (CR)** and **Average Variance Extracted (AVE)** values for each individual factor in the measurement model can be evaluated to further assess the reliability of the survey instrument.[33] The CR is a measure of the general reliability of heterogeneous but similar scale items, such that it measures the reliability of the latent variable (see Chapter 5). Unlike the Cronbach's Alpha (α), which measures the reliability of the observed variables together.[49] The AVE, on the other hand, assesses the amount of variance captured by a factor or construct as compared with the variance that occurs due to random measurement error. The value of the AVE for each construct should be ≥ **0.50**, while that of the CR should be ≥ **0.70**, though a value ≥ **0.60** is acceptable.[33, 52] In the event that the recommended thresholds for any of these criteria, namely the Cronbach's Alpha (α), CR and/ or AVE are not met, the researcher must revisit the EFA to ensure that these criteria are met before any further forms of analysis, especially Structural Equation Modelling, can be run using the data set.

Practical Demonstration of Reliability Tests

Procedure for generating Cronbach Alpha (a) in SPSS

1. Click **Analyze** > **Scale** > **Reliability Analysis** on the top menu, as shown below:

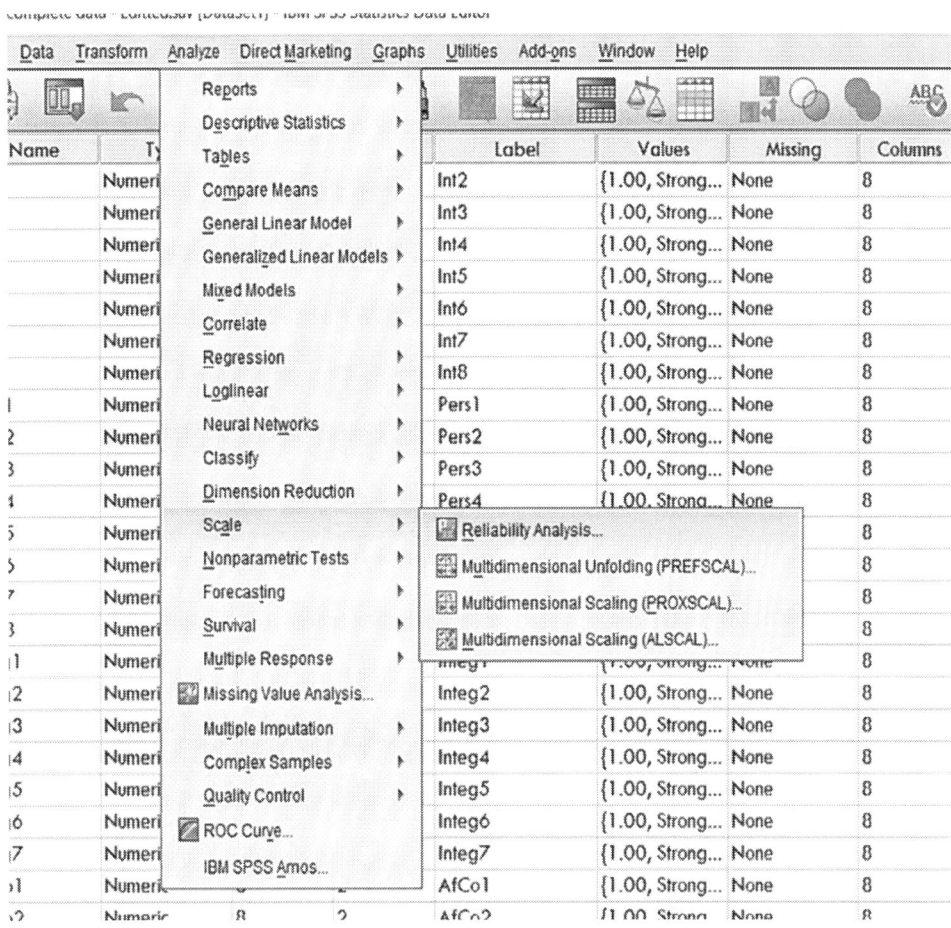

2. You will be presented with the **Reliability Analysis** dialogue box, as shown below:

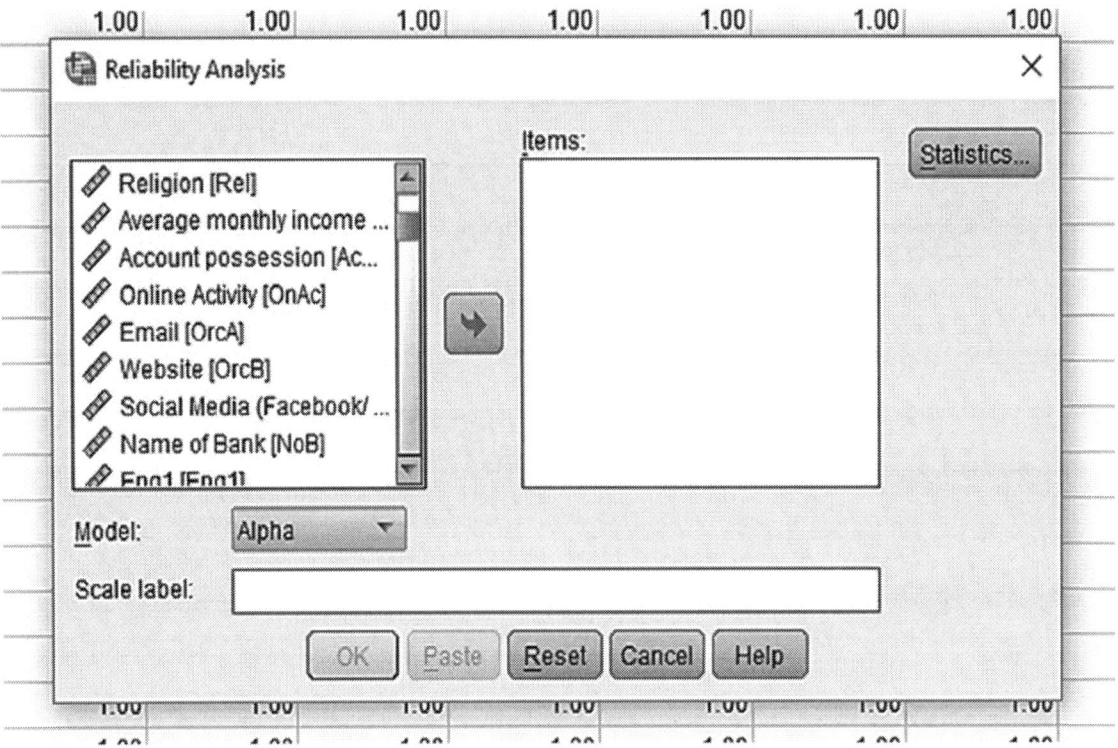

3. Transfer the variables that you want to check reliability for into the **Items** box by either dragging-and-dropping or using the arrow button, as seen below. In this example, we transfer the variables **Pers 3-6.**

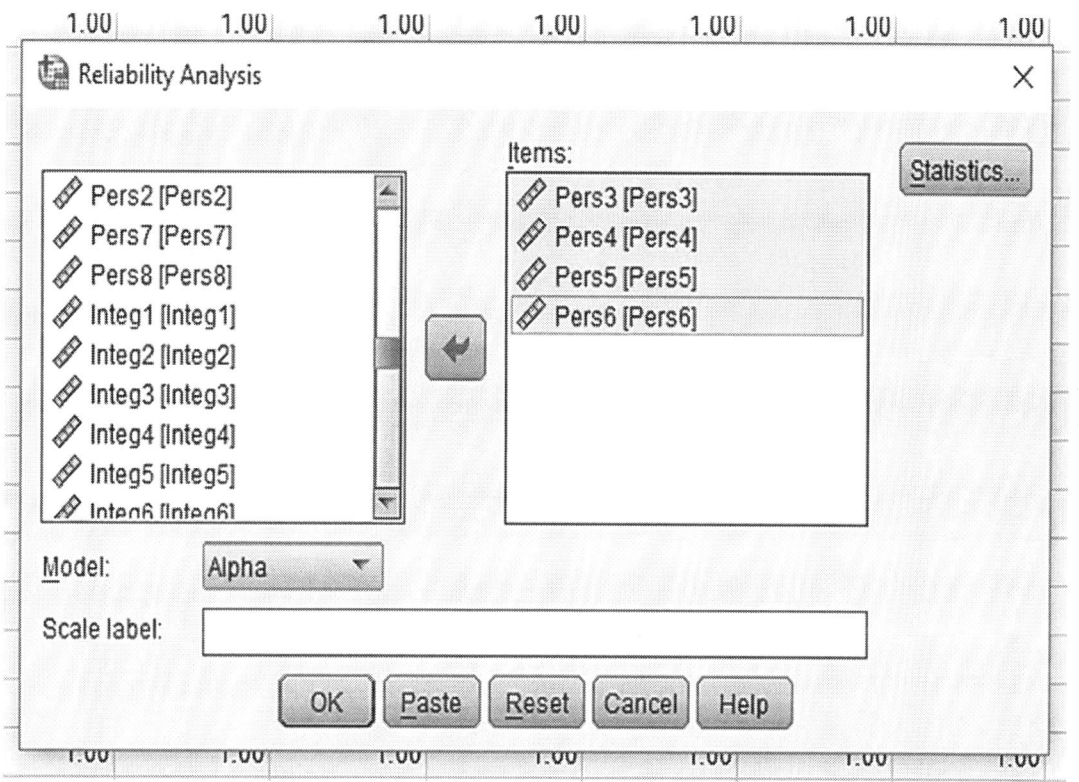

9. Click the **Statistics** button. You will be presented with the **Reliability Analysis: Statistics** dialogue box, as shown below.

   ❖ Select **Scale** and **Scale if item deleted** in the *Descriptives for* area.

   ❖ Leave **None** checked in the *ANOVA Table* area.

You will end up with a screen similar to the one below.

   ❖ Click **Continue**.

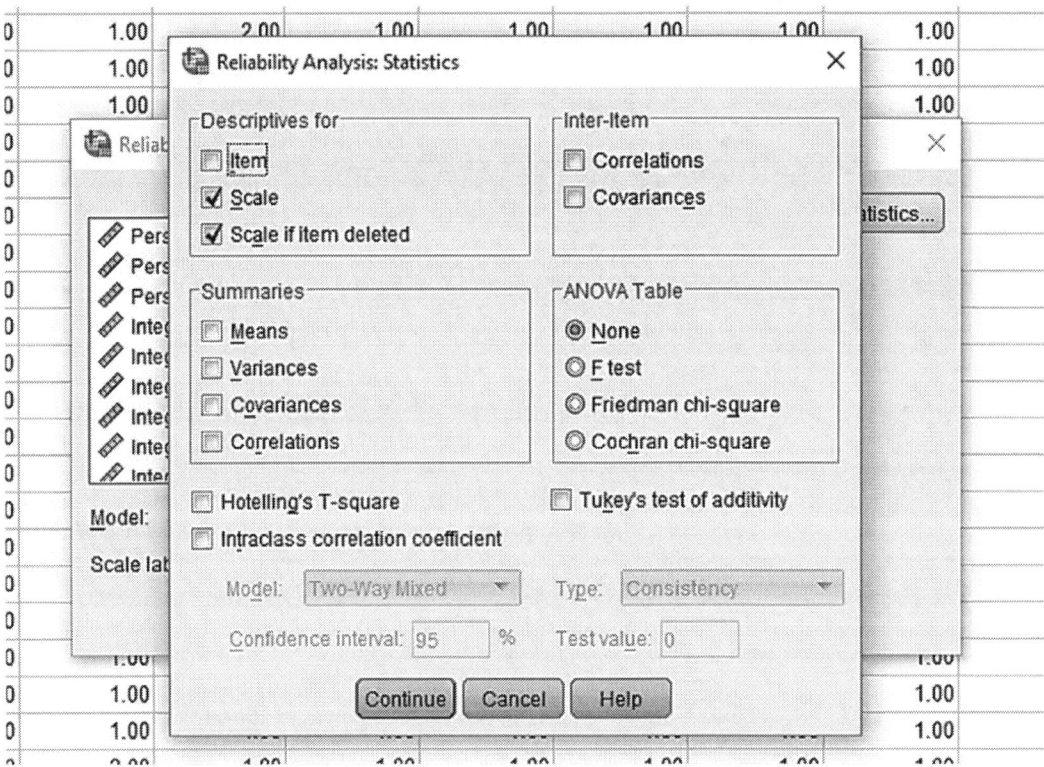

4. Ensure that **Alpha** is selected in the *Model* area, as shown below.

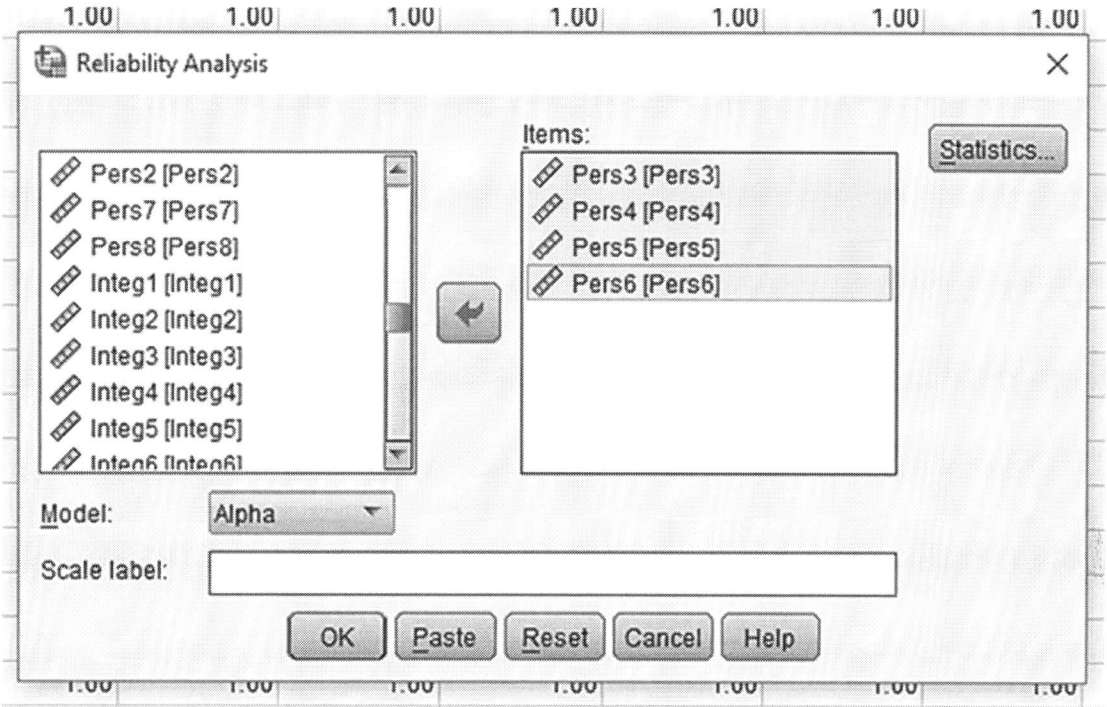

5. Click **OK** to generate the output.

SPSS Output Required

The output generated by SPSS provides pertinent information about your measurement scales for the given construct. However, the main output required is that of the **Reliability Statistics** and the **Item-Total Statistics**, as seen below.

Reliability Statistics

Cronbach's Alpha	N of Items
.900	4

Item-Total Statistics

	Scale Mean if Item Deleted	Scale Variance if Item Deleted	Corrected Item-Total Correlation	Cronbach's Alpha if Item Deleted
Pers3	10.6350	13.050	.645	.921
Pers4	10.0217	11.948	.859	.842
Pers5	9.8233	12.216	.838	.850
Pers6	9.8800	12.309	.782	.870

Analyzing the Output

First the most important value, the **Cronbach's Alpha** coefficient that is shown in the **Reliability Statistics** table is considered. In this example the value is 0.900, which is above 0.7.[45] Hence, the scale in our example can be considered to be reliable. Next the **Item-Total Statistics** Table is checked. Assuming the Cronbach's alpha value for the scale does not meet the requirements for acceptability (less than 0.6), the researcher may consider removing items with low item-total correlations; as presented in the column marked **Corrected Item-Total Correlation.** In the column labeled **Alpha if Item Deleted**, the impact of removing each item separately from the scale is provided. These are compared with the alpha value obtained and if any of the values in the **Alpha if Item Deleted** column are higher than the alpha value obtained in the **Reliability Statistics** table, the researcher might want to consider removing this item from the scale.

Procedure for generating Composite Reliability (CR) and Average Variance Extracted (AVE) values in Excel

1. Open a blank Excel spreadsheet and create the headings Composite Reliability (CR) and Average Variance Extracted (AVE) in the first row, as seen below. Note that there are distinct colors used to represent each measurement parameter. This is to aid in identifying which calculations relate to which parameter when conducting subsequent calculations.

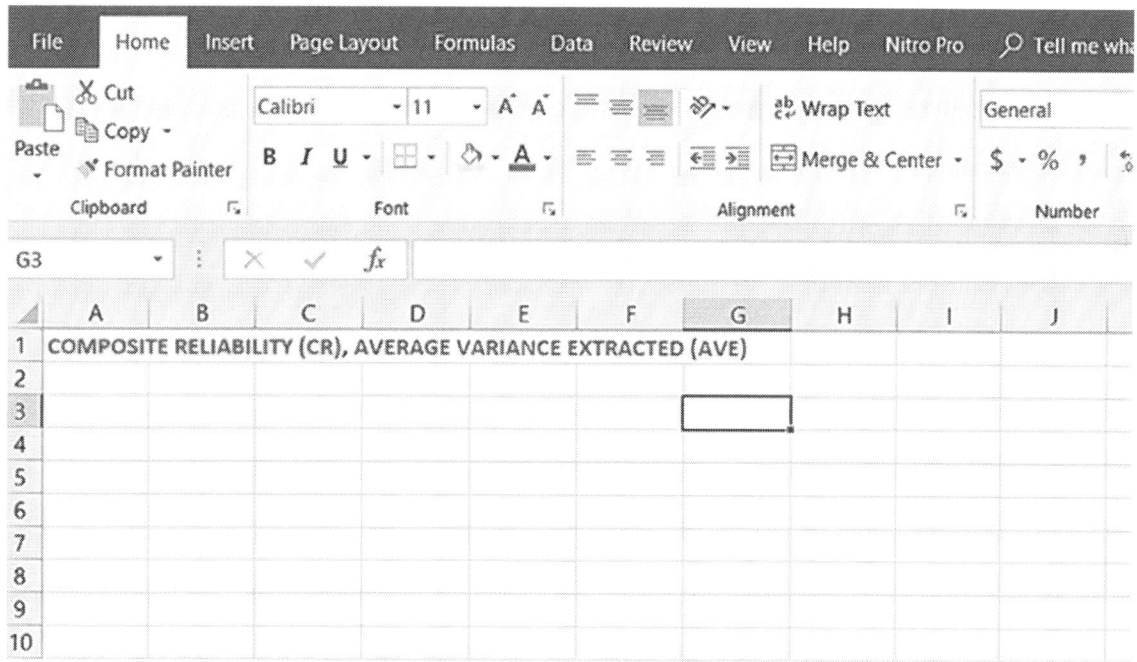

2. On row 3 insert the following, as seen below:

    - Under column B insert the Lambda (λ) symbol
    - Under column C insert Lambda squared ($λ^2$)
    - Under column D insert 1 minus Lambda squared ($1-λ^2$)

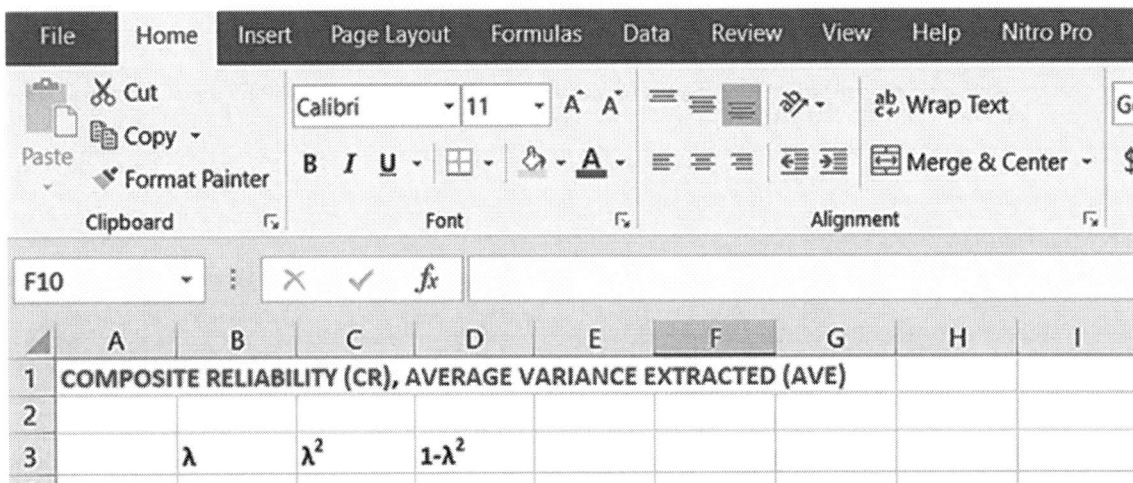

3. Copy the factor loadings for each of the items that make up the construct whose CR and AVE is to be calculated. In this example, we will calculate the CR and AVE for **Personalization**, which is represented by **Pers 3-6**. This is shown below:

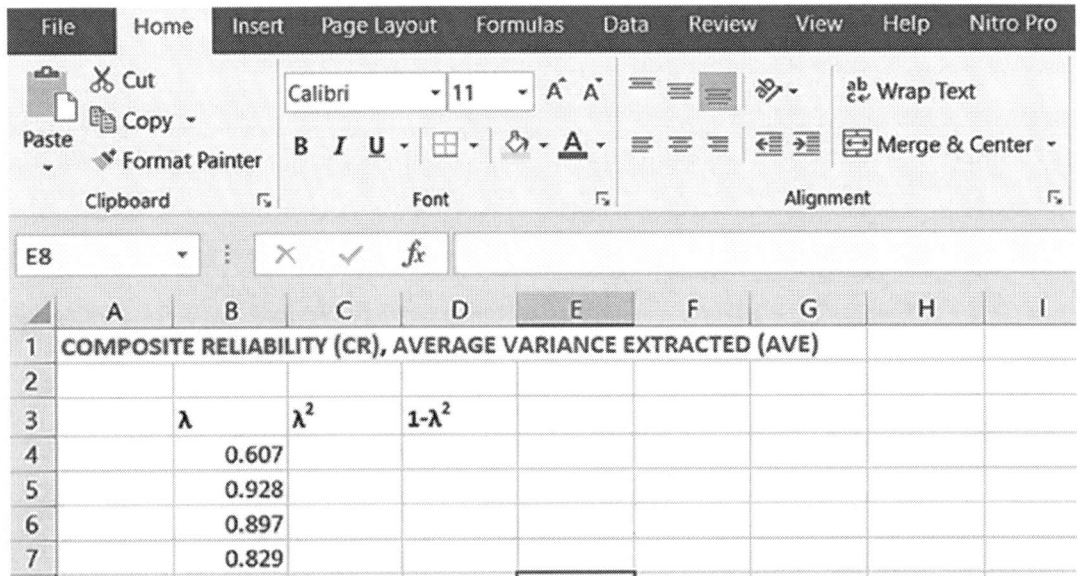

4. Compute the square of lambda on row **4** under column **C**, and drag down to replicate the formula in the remaining cells beneath it, as seen below:

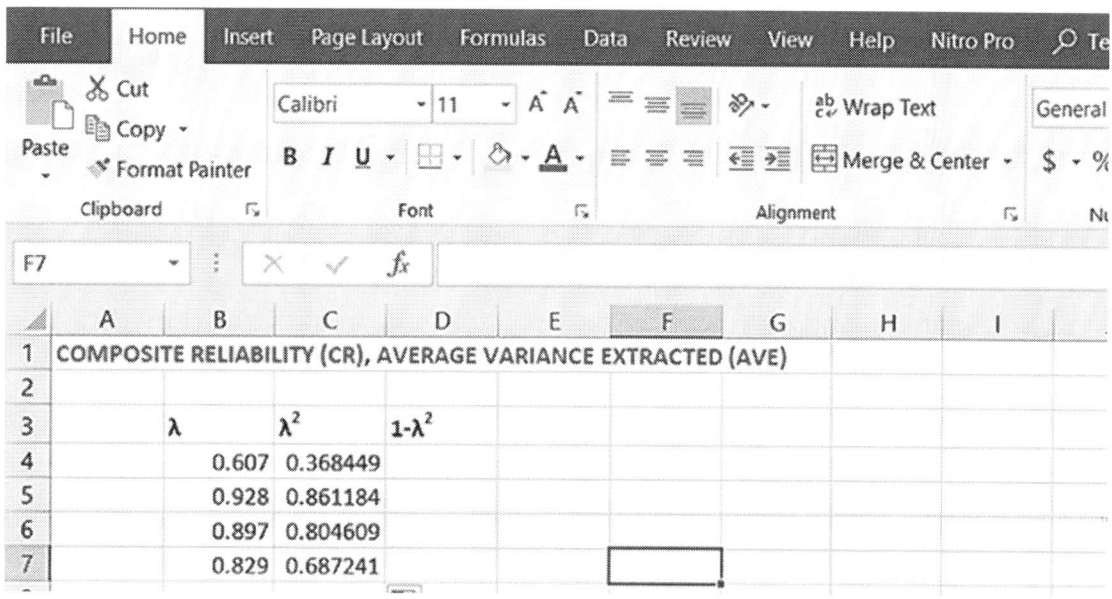

5. Compute 1 minus the square of lambda on row **4** under column **D**, and drag down to replicate the formula in the remaining cells beneath it, as seen below:

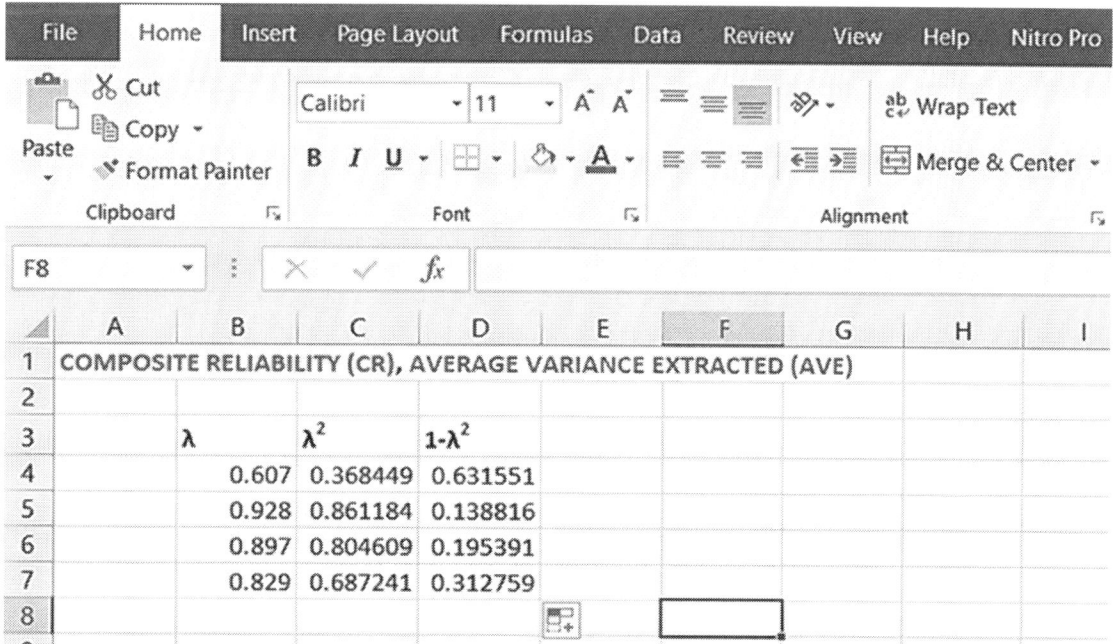

6. Under column **A** type the following, as shown below:
    - On row **9** type **COUNT**
    - On row **10** type **SUM**
    - On row **11** type **SQUARE**
    - On row **12** type **AVE**
    - On row **13** type **CR**

G18

	A	B	C	D	E	F	G	H
1	**COMPOSITE RELIABILITY (CR), AVERAGE VARIANCE EXTRACTED (AVE)**							
2								
3		**λ**	**$λ^2$**	**$1\text{-}λ^2$**				
4		0.607	0.368449	0.631551				
5		0.928	0.861184	0.138816				
6		0.897	0.804609	0.195391				
7		0.829	0.687241	0.312759				
8								
9	**COUNT**							
10	**SUM**							
11	**SQUARE**							
12	**AVE**							
13	**CR**							

7. Under column **A** compute the following, as shown below:
   - ❖ A count of all the items under λ, λ^2 and $1 - \lambda^2$ in columns **B, C** and **D**, into cells **B9, C9** and **D9**
   - ❖ A sum of all the items under λ, λ^2 and $1 - \lambda^2$ in columns **B, C** and **D**, into cells **B10, C10** and **D10**
   - ❖ A square of the sum of all the items under λ in cell **B10**, into cell **B11**

	A	B	C	D	E	F	G	H
1	COMPOSITE RELIABILITY (CR), AVERAGE VARIANCE EXTRACTED (AVE)							
2								
3		λ	λ^2	$1-\lambda^2$				
4		0.607	0.368449	0.631551				
5		0.928	0.861184	0.138816				
6		0.897	0.804609	0.195391				
7		0.829	0.687241	0.312759				
8								
9	COUNT	4	4	4				
10	SUM	3.261	2.721483	1.278517				
11	SQUARE	10.63412						
12	AVE							
13	CR							

8. Using the distinct colors for **Composite Reliability (CR)** and **Average Variance Extracted (AVE)** provided, indicate the measures that are going to be used in computing each parameter as shown below:

	A	B	C	D	E	F	G	H
1	COMPOSITE RELIABILITY (CR), AVERAGE VARIANCE EXTRACTED (AVE)							
2								
3		λ	λ^2	$1-\lambda^2$				
4		0.607	0.368449	0.631551				
5		0.928	0.861184	0.138816				
6		0.897	0.804609	0.195391				
7		0.829	0.687241	0.312759				
8								
9	COUNT	4	4	4				
10	SUM	3.261	2.721483	1.278517				
11	SQUARE	10.63412						
12	AVE							
13	CR							

9. Compute the AVE and CR values using the color codes provided, as seen below:

   1. For the **AVE** it's the value in cell **C10** (A sum of all the items under λ^2) divided by a count of all the items under $\lambda2$, in cell **C9** [**The average of the total squared loadings**]

   ❖ For the **CR** it's the value in cell **B11** (A square of the sum of all the items under λ in cell **B10**), divided by the value in cell **B11** + the value in cell **D10** (A sum of all the items under $1-\lambda^2$)

	A	B	C	D
1	COMPOSITE RELIABILITY (CR), AVERAGE VARIANCE EXTRACTED (AVE)			
2				
3		λ	λ^2	$1-\lambda^2$
4		0.607	0.368449	0.631551
5		0.928	0.861184	0.138816
6		0.897	0.804609	0.195391
7		0.829	0.687241	0.312759
8				
9	COUNT	4	4	4
10	SUM	3.261	2.721483	1.278517
11	SQUARE	10.63412		
12	AVE	0.680371		
13	CR	0.892676		
14				

Analyzing the Output

In this example we observe that the value for the AVE is 0.680, which is above the 0.5 threshold that is recommended in literature.[45] Also, the CR is 0.892, which is also clearly higher than the recommended cut-off point. The quantitative data analysis literature holds that CR should be ≥ 0.7 and AVE should be ≥ 0.5 for each construct.[33, 52] Hence, the measurement scale in our example can be considered to be reliable.

After the spreadsheet is set and used to test for the CR and AVE of a construct once, the same spreadsheet can be used to test for the CR and AVE values of all the remaining constructs in the model. This is done by simply replacing the factor loadings in the first column under λ with the factor loadings of the individual items that make up the next construct whose CR and AVE is to be determined. Subsequently, the outcome of the reliability test is presented in the form of a loadings table, as seen in Table 4.

TABLE 4 - LOADINGS TABLE[31]

Construct and measurement items	β	t-value (significance)	CR	AVE	α
Engagement			0.90	0.70	0.90
I "like" content posted on my bank's Facebook page	0.92	Fixed			
I retweet comments posted on my bank's Twitter handle	0.71	18.12***			
My bank's website has hotlinks to their Twitter/Facebook pages	0.87	26.45***			
Other customers provide helpful information on my bank's Facebook page	0.82	23.51***			
Interactivity			0.95	0.80	0.95
My bank has site navigation tools on their website	0.89	Fixed			
My bank's website has a search tool that enables me to locate items	0.93	30.50***			
I get the desired answers to my online enquiries	0.90	28.36***			
24-hour live chat/help is available on my bank's website	0.85	24.54***			
My bank's online platforms provide mechanisms that help me to evaluate and select appropriate products and services	0.90	28.36***			
Online trust			0.84	0.52	0.84
I can count on my bank to ensure that transactions carried out on its website are without error	0.81	Fixed			
I think that the information presented on my bank's website is reliable	0.78	17.28***			
My bank keeps customers' best interests in mind	0.57	11.95***			
I think that my bank would not do anything intentional on their website that would be unfair to customers	0.82	18.32***			
I feel like my privacy is protected while transacting with my bank online	0.60	12.59***			
Customer loyalty			0.86	0.55	0.85
I would be willing to pay a higher price for my bank's services over other banks	0.64	Fixed			
I prefer my bank to its competitors	0.74	12.57***			
My bank is the best bank for me	0.75	12.74***			
I would be willing to defend my bank in the face of any controversy	0.82	13.56***			
I would consider my bank as my first choice for patronizing banking services	0.77	12.99***			

Notes: $n = 429$. *** $p \leqslant 0.001$

Table 4 assesses the reliability of the measurement scales utilized in the study of Online Relationship Marketing (ORM) in the Ghanaian Banking Industry.[31] It shows the constructs studied in the research framework with their respective measurement items, along with their factor loadings and reliability diagnostics (Cronbach's Alpha (α), CR and AVE).

ASSESSING VALIDITY

There are two main types of validity that researchers need to assess when it comes to SEM. These are **Convergent validity** and **Discriminant validity**.[33]

1. **Convergent Validity**: It explains the extent to which individual measurement items that form a given construct share a high amount of variance in common. It captures the extent to which they make sense together.[50]

2. **Discriminant Validity**: It explains the degree to which a given construct is clearly distinct from other constructs in the framework or model under study. The constructs should be empirically distinguishable from each other.[53]

In assessing convergent validity, the Fornell and Larcker[54] criterion for convergent validity, as well as the Hair et al.[33] criteria for convergent validity are utilized. According to the Fornell and Larcker criterion, the AVE for each construct in the model must be greater than 0.5 in order to satisfy the requirement of convergent validity. Whereas, the Hair et al. criteria require not just that the AVE for each construct be greater than 0.5, but also for the standardized factor loadings of all the items that make up each construct to be not less than 0.5 and the CR for each construct to be not less than 0.6.[33] Nevertheless, the satisfaction of the reliability criteria discussed above, also counts as an indicator of convergent validity.

On the other hand, discriminant validity is evaluated by means of the Fornell and Larcker[54] criterion for discriminant validity. It requires that the AVE for each construct must be greater than the square of the corresponding inter-construct correlations. This is expressed using a correlation table that shows the squared correlations between the individual constructs studied in the framework, with their corresponding AVEs placed on the diagonal within the table, as presented in Table 5. It also includes a footnote at the bottom of the table, which explains the dimensions of the table and whether or not it satisfies the criteria for discriminant validity. [31]

TABLE 5 - CORRELATION MATRIX WITH AVEs[31]

Construct	1	2	3	4
1. Engagement	*0.70*			
2. Interactivity	0.50	*0.80*		
3. Online trust	0.34	0.62	*0.52*	
4. Customer loyalty	0.10	0.09	0.24	*0.55*
Mean	2.5	3.5	4.1	4.0
SD	1.2	1.2	0.7	0.7

Notes: Average variances extracted (AVE) are on the diagonal (in italic); squared correlations are off-diagonal. The AVEs for each construct are far greater than the corresponding inter-construct square correlations, thereby supporting discriminant validity

CHAPTER SUMMARY

In this chapter readers were provided with a breakdown of the different dimensions of construct reliability and validity in quantitative analysis. They learned how to compute reliability, convergent and discriminant validity criteria in SPSS and Microsoft Excel, namely Cronbach's Alpha (α), AVE and CR. How to present and interpret this output was also addressed. The next chapter will discuss the basics of structural equation modelling to give readers a foundational understanding of the technique.

Chapter Review

Question 1

How do quantitative journal articles in your field of study address reliability and validity issues? Discuss.

Chapter 7

Structural Equation Modelling (SEM) - The Basics

OBJECTIVES

The chapter seeks to introduce readers to the basics of structural equation modelling. It discusses what structural equation modelling is all about, as well as its advantages over other similar forms of quantitative data analysis. SEM nomenclature and SEM notation are also examined, in addition to the fundamental building blocks required to put together a good structural equation modelling analysis.

What is Structural Equation Modelling (SEM)?

SEM is a statistical modeling technique which is a combination of factor analysis and regression or path analysis. Also known as latent variable path analysis or causal modeling, SEM allows for the simultaneous investigation of direct and indirect causal relationships between latent (unobserved) constructs that are measured by several observed variables (see Chapter 5). SEM enables researchers to conduct complex, multidimensional, and more precise analysis of empirical data considering different aspects of the examined reality, as well as the abstract concepts or theoretical constructs.[56] As a result, it can be viewed as an amalgamation of regression analysis that includes systems of simultaneous equations and factor analysis. It consists of a series of multiple regression equations that are all fitted at the same time. SEM's capability for simultaneous analysis greatly differs from most first-generation statistical methods such as Linear regression, Logistic regression, and Analysis of Variance (ANOVA), which analyze only one layer of the linkages between independent and dependent variables at a time.

There are several advantages to using SEM for model testing rather than other statistical methods. Among others:

1. SEM enables researchers to study intricate patterns of relationships among the constructs in a conceptual model in an integrative manner.
2. Researchers are able to measure latent (unobserved) variables using observed variables, considering the effect of measurement error on the structural relationships that exist between them.
3. SEM helps researchers resolve problems of multicollinearity, by identifying unique groups of observed variables to represent separate latent variables.
4. SEM analysis simultaneously produces model fit indices in addition to individual parameter estimates.

5. SEM software (Amos) provides a graphical representation of the multiple equations in a given model that gives researchers a convenient way to view and present complex relationships among variables.

SEM Nomenclature

SEM adopts a slightly different naming system for variables. This is because variables in a given SEM analysis may influence one-another reciprocally, either directly or through other variables as intermediaries.[57] Therefore, using dependent and independent variables makes less sense in this context, given that the dependent variable in one equation might be an independent variable in another equation. For this reason, SEM identifies two main types of latent variables: **Endogenous** and **Exogenous**. **Endogenous latent variables** are the outcomes or the result from the influences of other variables (exogenous variables), thus they usually have at least one single-headed arrow pointing towards them. Each endogenous latent variable is assigned with a unique residual term (as explained in the next paragraph). This is because there is the need to account for the amount of measurement error captured by the exogenous variables in predicting the endogenous variable in question. Also, it distinguishes the endogenous variables from the exogenous variables. **Exogenous latent variables** are the variables that cause changes or have an influence on other variables in a model. Thus, they usually have at least one single-headed arrow pointing away from them. Nonetheless, endogenous variables can also predict or affect other variables in the model, as exogenous variables. Hence, they can additionally have at least one single-headed arrow also pointing out of them.

More so, SEM also identifies **disturbances** or **residuals**. All the observed variables in a given model are assumed to be tainted by some form of random measurement error, this is because what the researcher observes and measures may not always equate what was initially predicted. Thus, each measurement item contains some random measurement error that must be accounted for and this is referred to as a residual. These are presented for each of the observed variables in the conceptual model (see Figure 5).

SEM Notation

FIGURE 5 - SEM NOTATION IN AMOS

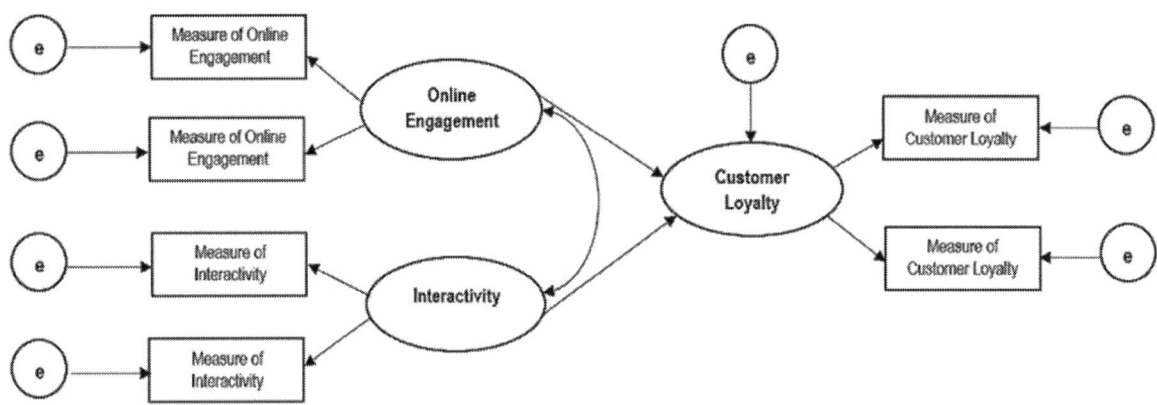

In Amos, **ellipses** are used to represent latent (unobserved) variables, while **rectangular boxes** are used to represent observed variables A **single-headed arrow** from an ellipse to a rectangular box represents a *measurement relationship*, whereas a single-headed arrow between two ellipses represents a **causal relationship**. Also, a **double-headed arrow** between two shapes, on the other hand represents a **non-causal (unexplained) relationship**, this is called covariance. **Covariances** depict the manner in which two variables are linearly related, such that changes in one are associated with changes in the other. Residuals are also identified in the model; using a **circle** with a small **'e'** in the middle. A **single-headed arrow** from one of these circles to a rectangular box represents the residual for that particular observed variable. These are all depicted in Figure 5 above. The figure presents a model of the effect of online engagement and interactivity on customer loyalty. It shows both latent and observed variables, with their corresponding relationships as presented for SEM analysis.

Performing SEM Analysis

In performing SEM analysis there are certain stages that researchers must follow. These stages are required in order to successfully complete a SEM analysis and achieve good results. These constitute the basic building blocks of SEM, as presented in the diagram below.[59]

FIGURE 6 - SEM BUILDING BLOCKS

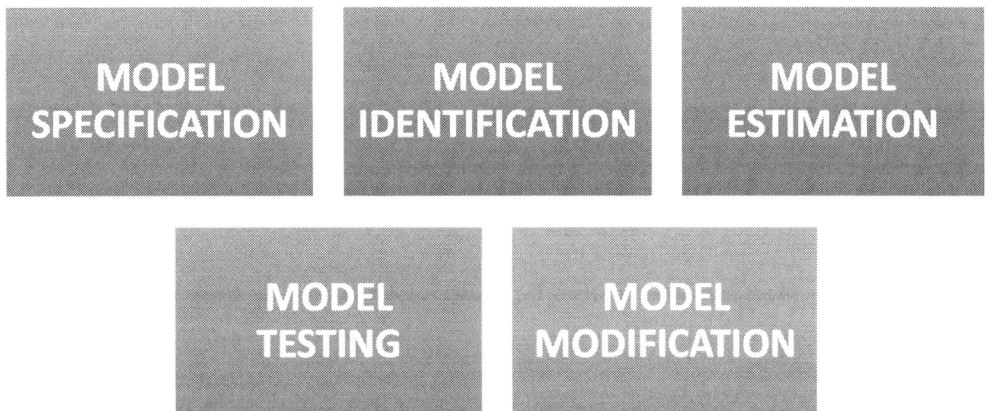

Model Specification

Every SEM analysis begins with a good theoretically based research model. Prior to any data collection and analysis activity, the researcher must specify a research model, deciding on which variables should and should not be included in the model. Additionally, the researcher must decide on how these variables are related to each other, primarily on the basis of theoretical considerations. The inclusion of variables that are theoretically irrelevant in a model and/ or the exclusion of variables that are theoretically relevant from a model leads to what is called a **misspecified model**, which causes specification error.[59] This can lead to a number of consequences, including biased parameter estimates and a lack of fit between the model and the data gathered. However, there are some procedures available for researchers to detect specification error to aid them in obtaining a more correctly specified model, which are discussed in the sections on model testing and model modification.

Model Identification

Model identification refers to the possibility of identifying one unique value for each of the parameters in the research model, using the observed data set.[60] However, there is an infinite number of probable solutions to this, especially in SEM where model identification is not so easily achieved. But, in order to solve this problem every possible parameter in the research model under study must be specified to be either **free**, **fixed** or **constrained**.[59] A free parameter is a parameter that is not known and therefore needs to be estimated. While, a fixed parameter is a parameter that is fixed to a specific value, typically either 0 or 1. Whereas, a constrained parameter that is not known, but is constrained to equal one or more of the other parameters in the research model. For the purposes of this guide to SEM analysis, a combination of free and fixed parameters is used in an attempt to achieve model identification. The item with the fixed parameter is referred to as the **marker variable**.

Model Estimation

The researcher at this stage has to choose a method by which to estimate the parameters in the research model. The most frequently used estimation methods in SEM include **Ordinary least squares (OLS)** also called unweighted least squares, **Generalized least squares (GLS)** and **Maximum likelihood (ML);** all of which can be done in Amos. OLS is the simplest and computationally easiest estimation method, while GLS is computationally more challenging and ML is computationally more thorough. In this guide to SEM analysis, the Maximum Likelihood (ML) estimation method is used, since it assumes multivariate normality among the observed variables, which leads to more efficient inferences. Using the ML method, the researcher is able to obtain estimates of the unknown parameters, such that the values obtained maximize the likelihood that the phenomenon described by the model produced the data that was actually gathered.

Model Testing

Model testing follows the model identification. After the researcher has obtained the parameter estimates for a given research model using SEM, the next step is to ascertain how well the data gathered fits with the research model. Here the researcher seeks to answer the question, *"To what extent is the research model supported by the sample data gathered?"* To answer this question there are two main tests that are utilized. The researcher must consider the **model fit** criteria, as well as the **individual parameter estimates** of the model. Unlike other statistical techniques like multiple regression, which has one very strong determinant of model fit (the F test statistic), in SEM there are several indices with which we can determine model fit. These are discussed in the ensuing section.

Model Fit Indices

Good model fit is the first necessity in model testing. Several researchers suggest various indices by which researchers can assess the adequacy of both the measurement model and the structural model in a given study, using various cut-off criteria.[61,62] These indices are broadly classified into three main groups that reflect **Absolute fit**, **Comparative fit** and **Parsimonious fit**. Each index with their respective cut-off points are depicted in Figure 7 and explained as follows.

- **Absolute/ Predictive fit indices**

  This set of indices examine the closeness of fit. They provide a basic assessment of how well the researcher's theory fits with the data gathered.[37] Some indices commonly used in checking for absolute fit include the **Chi-square (χ^2)** statistic (this called **CMIN** in Amos), **Goodness-of-fit index (GFI)**, **Adjusted Goodness-of-fit index (AGFI)**, the **Root Mean Square Error of Approximation (RMSEA)** and the **Standardized Root Mean Square Residual (SRMR)**.

• Comparative/ Incremental fit indices

This set of indices compare the fit of the model under consideration with an estimated baseline-model.[63] The most commonly utilized baseline model is the null model, which assumes that all the observed variables are uncorrelated. There are several indices that fall within this set, including the **Comparative Fit Index (CFI)**, **the Incremental Fit Index (IFI)** and the **Tucker-Lewis Index (TLI)**.

FIGURE 7 - CUT-OFF CRITERIA FOR FIT INDICES[62]

Indexes	Shorthand	General rule for acceptable fit if data are continuous	Categorical data
Absolute/predictive fit			
Chi-square	χ^2	Ratio of χ^2 to $df \leq 2$ or 3, useful for nested models/model trimming	
Akaike information criterion	AIC	Smaller the better; good for model comparison (nonnested), not a single model	
Browne–Cudeck criterion	BCC	Smaller the better; good for model comparison, not a single model	
Bayes information criterion	BIC	Smaller the better; good for model comparison (nonnested), not a single model	
Consistent AIC	CAIC	Smaller the better; good for model comparison (nonnested), not a single model	
Expected cross-validation index	ECVI	Smaller the better; good for model comparison (nonnested), not a single model	
Comparative fit		Comparison to a baseline (independence) or other model	
Normed fit index	NFI	$\geq .95$ for acceptance	
Incremental fit index	IFI	$\geq .95$ for acceptance	
Tucker–Lewis index	TLI	$\geq .95$ can be $0 > TLI > 1$ for acceptance	0.96
Comparative fit index	CFI	$\geq .95$ for acceptance	0.95
Relative noncentrality fit index	RNI	$\geq .95$, similar to CFI but can be negative, therefore CFI better choice	
Parsimonious fit			
Parsimony-adjusted NFI	PNFI	Very sensitive to model size	
Parsimony-adjusted CFI	PCFI	Sensitive to model size	
Parsimony-adjusted GFI	PGFI	Closer to 1 the better, though typically lower than other indexes and sensitive to model size	
Other			
Goodness-of-fit index	GFI	$\geq .95$ Not generally recommended	
Adjusted GFI	AGFI	$\geq .95$ Performance poor in simulation studies	
Hoelter .05 index		Critical N largest sample size for accepting that model is correct	
Hoelter .01 index		Hoelter suggestion, $N = 200$, better for satisfactory fit	
Root mean square residual	RMR	Smaller, the better; 0 indicates perfect fit	
Standardized RMR	SRMR	$\leq .08$	
Weighted root mean residual	WRMR	$< .90$	$< .90$
Root mean square error of approximation	RMSEA	$< .06$ to .08 with confidence interval	$< .06$

- **Parsimonious fit indices**

This set of indices enable the researcher to determine which model out of a set of competing models is the best, in terms of complexity.[37] A measure of parsimony fit can be improved by either a better model fit or a simpler model. Examples of these indices include the **Parsimony-adjusted Normed Fit Index (PNFI)** and the **Parsimony-adjusted Comparative Fit Index (PCFI)**.

Individual Parameter Estimates

The estimates for each of the individual parameters are considered next. Here, three main features are considered:

1. The **critical value (CR)** of each parameter estimated should exceed the expected value at a specified Alpha (α) level. For instance, at $\alpha = 0.05$ in a two tailed test, the ***t* value** for each parameter must be ≥ 1.96, as applied in this guide to SEM.

2. The **sign of the estimated parameter**, whether negative or positive must correspond with what is expected from the theoretical model. For example, if the expectation is that higher online engagement will lead to higher customer loyalty, then an estimate with a positive sign will support that expectation.

3. The individual parameter estimates should all be ≥ 0.5 and be theoretically sound, in order to facilitate meaningful interpretation.

Model Modification

Modification seems to be necessary for all SEM models. This is because they rarely pass the test of model fit in the initial stages. In instances where the fit of the model tested is not as strong as should be, the researcher must modify and respecify the model, then subsequently evaluate the new modified model to ascertain its fit with the data obtained. This is referred to as a **specification search**, where the researcher is searching for a model that has a better fit and yields parameters that have practical significance. This search process is however, rarely stated as part of the research report. To be able to adequately and appropriately modify the model, there are certain procedures available to aid in the detection and rectification of specification errors.[59] The researcher can:

1. Examine the statistical significance of each parameter estimated in the model, and remove all parameters that are not statistically significant. The researcher must however note that because statistical significance is related to sample size; some parameters may be significant with a larger sample, but be insignificant with a small sample.

2. Also, examine the modification indices, which are produced as part of the CFA analysis output. These indices suggest remedies for the discrepancies between the proposed model and the estimated model. For instance, the presence of large modification indices indicates the presence of measurement items or variables loading on more than one factor, as well as error covariances.[64] These must be identified and systematically eliminated, one at a time, while evaluating the changes in the fit of the model till an acceptable level of model fit is achieved.

Ultimately, it is clear that there is no single procedure sufficient enough to find a correctly specified model. Nevertheless, researchers can apply the methods identified above, guided most importantly by theory, as well as practical considerations.

Chapter Summary

In this chapter the basics of structural equation modelling were introduced. Readers learned what structural equation modelling is and its advantages over other similar forms of quantitative data analysis such as multiple regression. SEM nomenclature and SEM notation were also examined, in addition to the basic principles of SEM analysis including model specification, model identification, model estimation and model modification. The ensuing chapter further expatiates on how to perform SEM analysis using the two-stage approach in Amos.

Chapter 8

Structural Equation Modelling (SEM) - The Two-Stage Approach

OBJECTIVES

This chapter aims to assist readers to develop a good conceptual and theoretical understanding of SEM and gain the ability to use in their own independent research. The chapter covers an array of topics, including the two-step approach to SEM analysis, the foundational concepts of measurement models, structural models, Confirmatory Factor Analysis (CFA) and Path Analysis (PA). It also teaches how to run SEM analysis using Amos, and how to interpret the resulting output. Alternative model comparison is also discussed.

WHY THE TWO-STAGE APPROACH?

The Two-stage approach to SEM, recommended by Anderson and Gerbing[65], has been used by several researchers in conducting their research.[58,66] This approach to SEM is recommended because prior to evaluating the causal relationships between the variables in a path analysis at the structural stage, there is the need for the researcher to ascertain the reliability and the validity of each construct, as well as their measurement items, using confirmatory factor analysis at the measurement stage. Hence, SEM is best conducted in two stages, in order to avoid any interaction between the measurement model and the structural model, which are produced at the measurement and structural stages of the approach respectively. These two stages, namely the **Measurement Stage** and the **Structural Stage** are discussed in the subsequent paragraphs.

Stage 1 - Measurement Stage

This stage involves the specification of the ***Measurement model***, with the primary aim of proving the unidimensionality of the measurement items for each individual construct, as well as their reliability and validity. This is because the researcher needs to ensure that each measurement item actually measures the construct that they are purported to and measure that construct alone. Thus, measurement items that load together on a scale are required to express variations in the same underlying construct. All this is achieved by means of a ***Confirmatory Factor Analysis (CFA)***, which is subsequently demonstrated. The CFA follows the performance of an initial Exploratory Factor Analysis (EFA) that is conducted specifically to obtain output that will be later used in performing a SEM analysis, as demonstrated in Chapter 5.

What is Confirmatory Factor Analysis (CFA)?

Confirmatory Factor Analysis (CFA) is a multivariate statistical technique that is similar to EFA, only that EFA is largely 'exploratory' and CFA is more 'confirmatory'. Using EFA, the manner in which the variables relate and are grouped based on inter-variable correlations (factor structure) is determined by running the software and allowing the underlying pattern of the data to ascertain the factor structure. Nonetheless, with CFA the determination of the factor structure is theory based. The researcher must indicate the number of constructs that exist for the set of variables entered, as well as the variables that load on each factor prior to running the analysis.[37] Hence, unlike EFA, CFA does not assign variables to factors, it rather confirms the position of variables under specific factors based on the theoretical pattern provided by the EFA or by the researcher. Simply put, in EFA the factor structure in the data set is explored; whereas in the CFA the factor structure that was extracted in the EFA or provided by the researcher is confirmed.

The accuracy of the resulting measurement model after the CFA, is assessed using the standardised regression weights (factor loadings) of each of the individual measurement items and their significance levels, as well as the fit indices of the model. In the situation where the model does not satisfy any of the criteria above, the researcher must modify the model to ensure that all criteria are satisfied. This is experienced in instances where the analysis produces factor loadings less than 0.5, insignificant factor loadings or does not produce a good- fitting model, in addition to producing unacceptable CR and AVE values. Model modification as discussed in Chapter 7 is utilised under these circumstances. Once all the criteria for factor loadings, significance level and model fit are satisfied, the researcher must proceed to assess the reliability, convergent validity and discriminant validity of the resulting constructs, as demonstrated in Chapter 6.

Stage 2 - Structural Stage

This stage involves the specification of the *Structural model*, with the primary aim of showing how the individual constructs relate to each other. It involves substituting the non-structural covariances between the latent variables with the hypothesized structure that is of main interest to the researcher and reanalysing the data. This hypothesised structure is used to test the proposed relationships that exist between the constructs, as espoused in the research framework. This is achieved by means of a ***Path Analysis (PA)***. Here, the overall suitability of the resulting structural model is determined by means of goodness-of-fit indices, as well as the significance levels and parameter estimates of the individual paths between the constructs, now clearly identified as either endogenous or exogenous variables.

What is Path Analysis (PA)?

Path Analysis (PA) is a multivariate statistical technique that is used to examine causal relationships between two or more variables in a set of simultaneous regression equations.[55] This approach is used by researchers who seek to understand the comparative strengths of direct and indirect relationships among a group of variables. In its uniqueness, path analysis has the ability to examine mediated pathways through specific variables, as well as multiple predictions of multiple variables in a model, unlike other linear equation modelling techniques such as multiple regression.

These two stages are illustrated in the ensuing practical demonstration section, using Amos software.

Amos Software

The Analysis of Moment Structures (Amos) software will be used in this guide to explore the structural inter-relationships among a set of variables. As mentioned earlier there are a number of other software that can be used to run a SEM analysis. However, Amos is recommended; especially for researchers who are new to the SEM technique for a number of reasons:

1. The software is visually easy to use.
2. It is easy to view and modify the measurement and structural models once they have been specified.
3. Amos produces tabular output that is similar to that of SPSS, which make the output easy to report and interpret.

4. It also produces publication-quality graphics.
5. Using Amos, we are further able to test all of the following simultaneously, namely model fit, individual parameter estimates, means and variances.

The Amos graphics graphical user interface, as observed in the practical demonstration depicts several tabs which provide various ways by which a researcher can execute different statistical commands. These are further discussed in the subsequent sections.

Practical Demonstration of the Two-Stage Approach to SEM

A researcher run a survey among 600 retail bank customers in order to determine if their loyalty to their primary bank was influenced by their level of engagement, personalized interactions with their bank online, as well as their calculative commitment to their bank (i.e., these are the four main constructs we are interested in). The questions in the survey were phrased such that customers' loyalty was captured by **BehLo 1-7**, the level of engagement with their bank online was captured as **Eng 1-7** and the questions coded as **Pers 1-8** represented the personalized interactions between the bank and their customers online. The procedure for analyzing the data set using the Two-Stage Approach to SEM is presented overleaf.

Procedure for Stage 1 - Measurement Stage using Amos

1. Open the Amos Graphics graphical interface, the screen below will open:

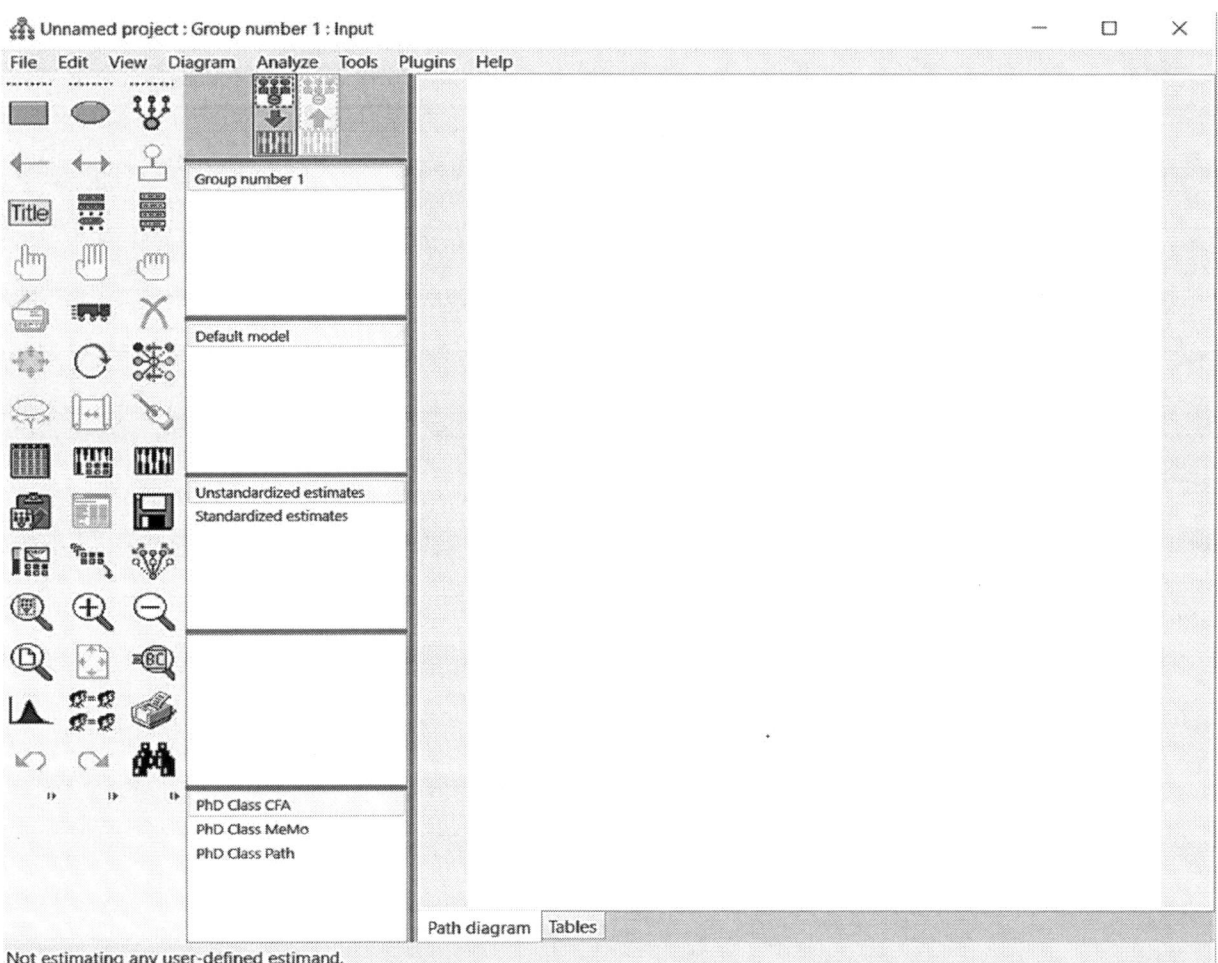

2. In the far-left corner of the screen various tabs are presented on a tool bar. These can be used to manually draw and estimate path diagrams. However, given the relative complexity of the models tested by researchers of late, more recent versions of Amos software have been created with plugins to expedite the analysis process by making it easier to draw path diagrams, draw covariances, name unobserved variables among others. These plugins are shown at the top of the screen under the heading **Plugins**, as shown below. If your version of Amos does not come with the plugins, you can access them from the internet and get them installed.

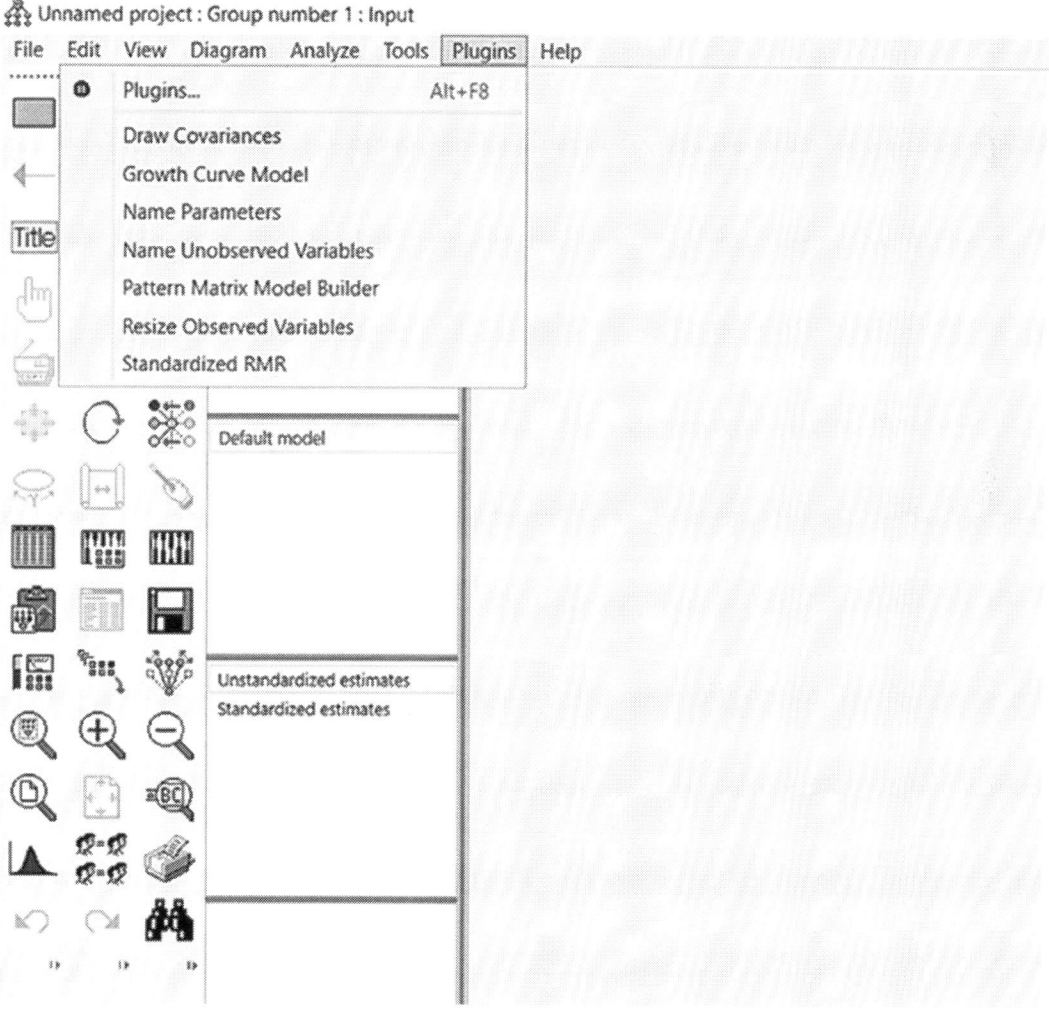

3. Before a model can be drawn or created, the data file must first be imported from SPSS into Amos. To achieve this:
    - ❖ Click the **Select data file(s)** tab, as seen below.
    - ❖ You will be presented with the **Data files** dialogue box, as shown below.
    - ❖ Click on **File Name** and navigate to the location where the data file is stored and select it. By default, Amos searches for a **.sav** file.

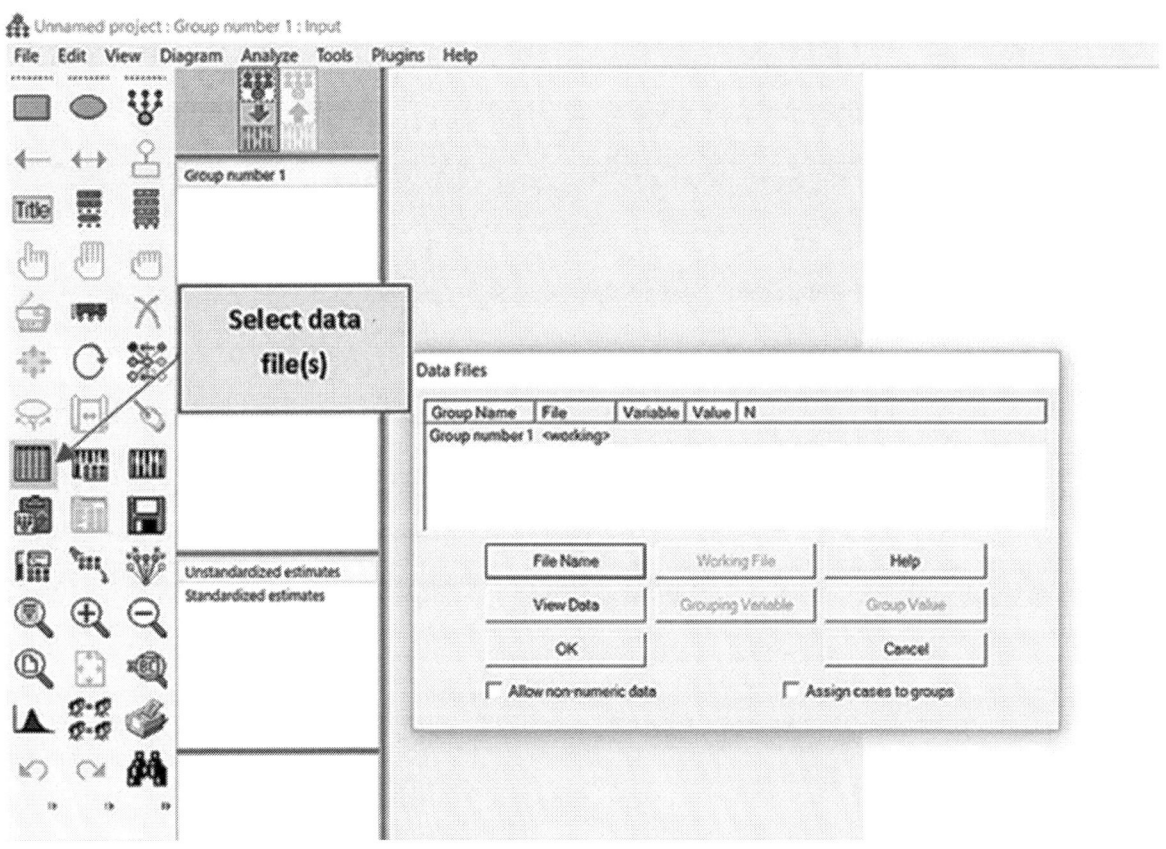

4. Choose the data file you wish to open, Click **Open**, then Click **OK**, as shown below:

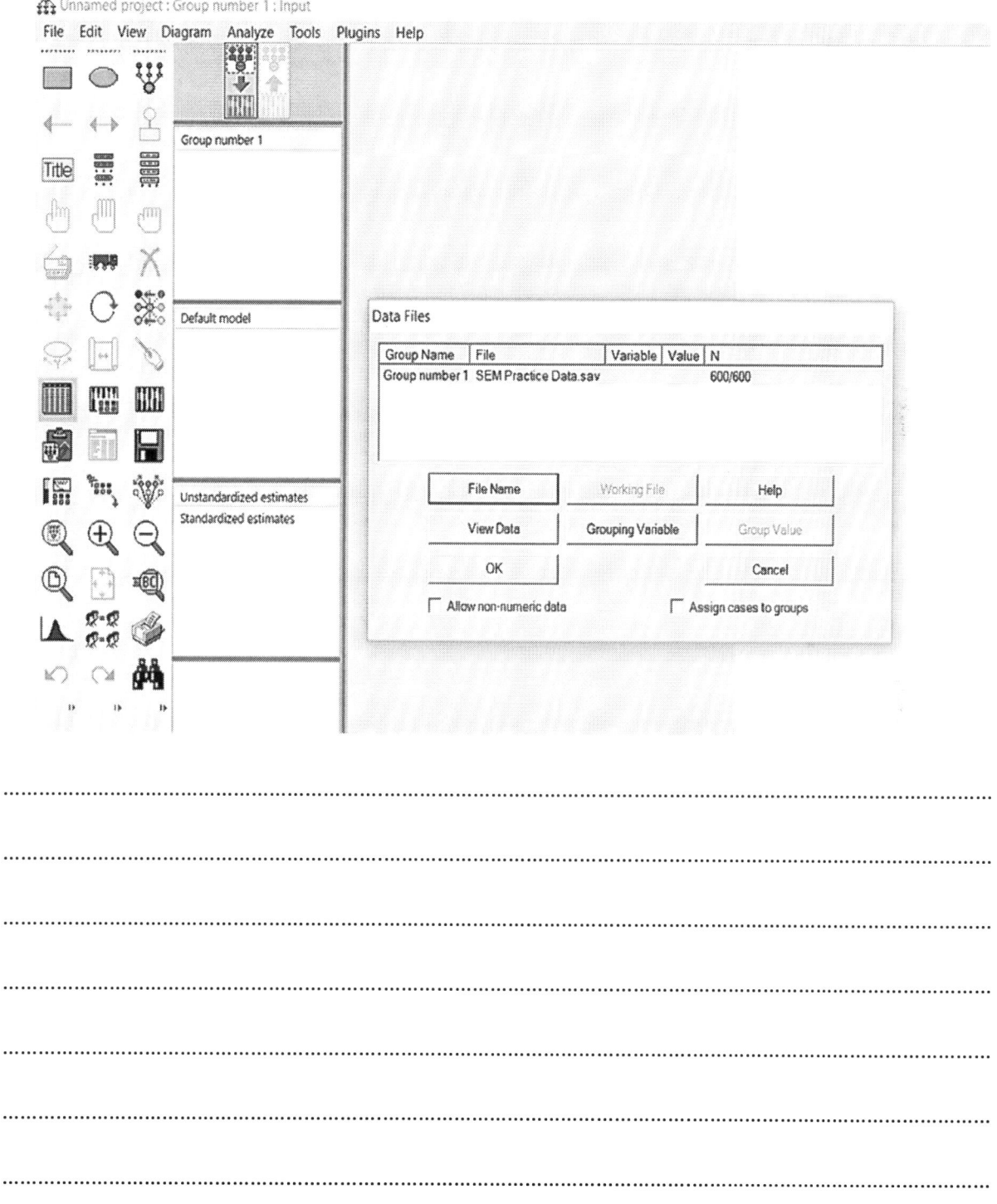

5. The next step is to create the path diagram. First click on **Pattern Matrix Model Builder** under the **Plugins** tab, as seen in Step 2 above. You will be presented with **the Pattern Matrix Input** box, as presented below.

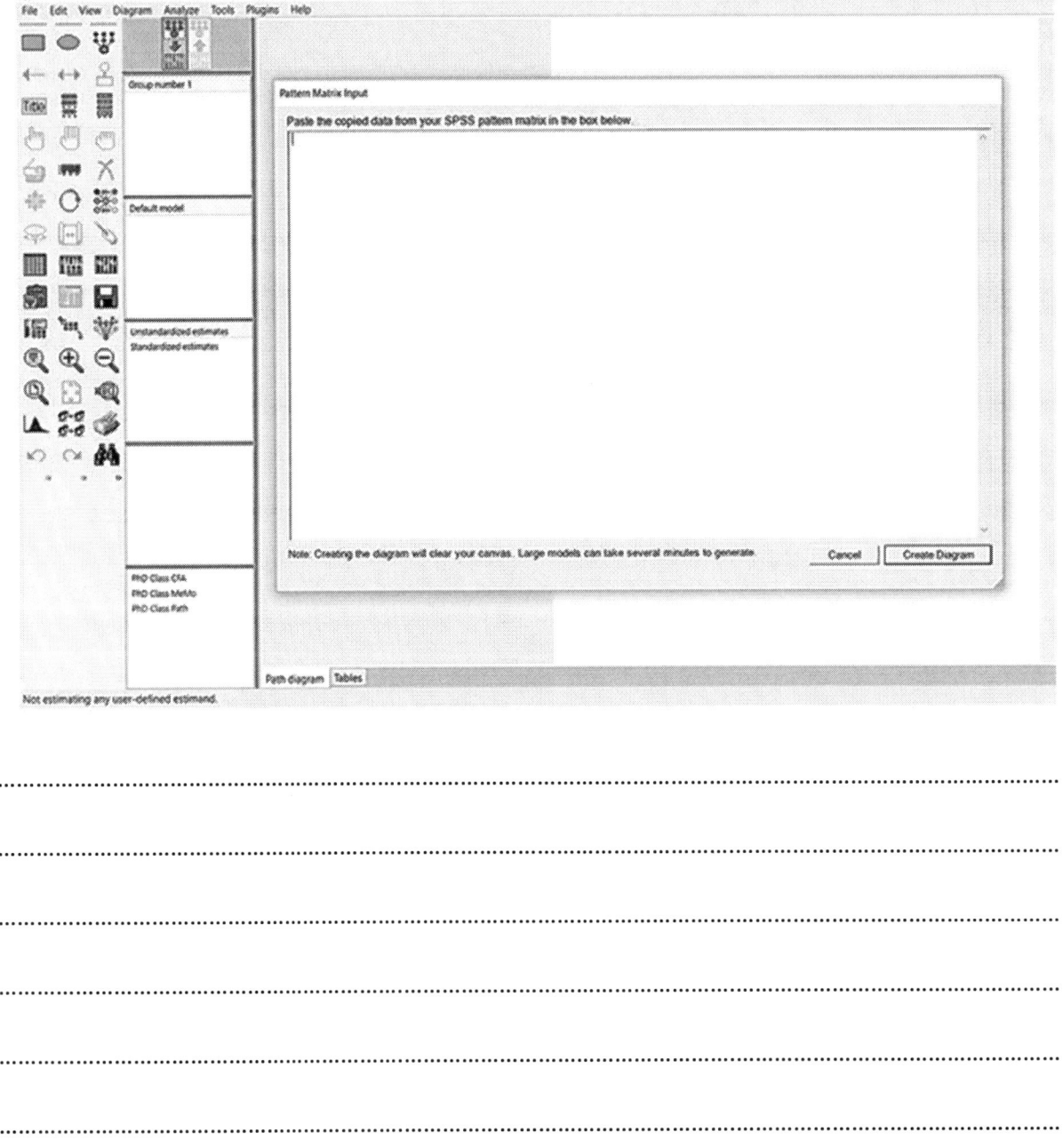

6. Copy the **Pattern Matrix** from the preliminary EFA analysis performed, as discussed in Chapter 5, right click in the **Pattern Matrix Input** box and paste it, like in the diagram below. Click **Create Diagram**, and wait a few minutes as the path diagram is being created.

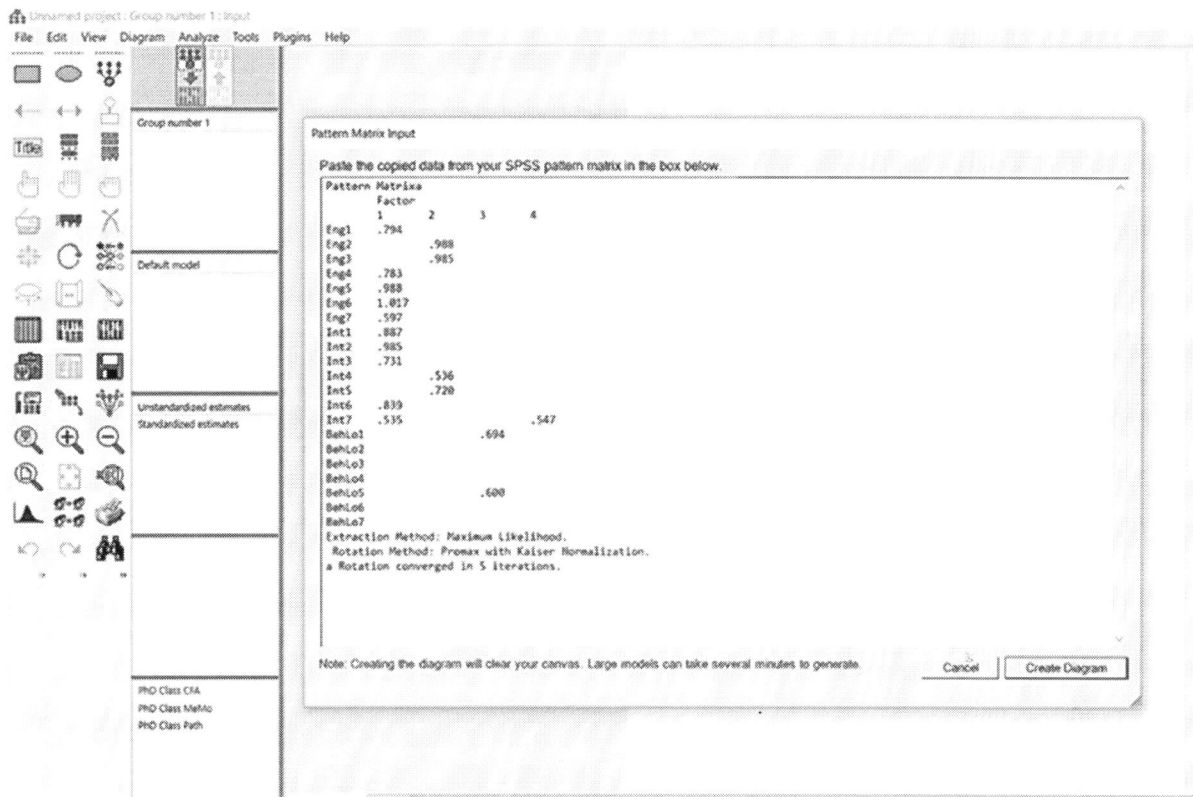

7. This creates an initial path diagram like the one below. Here you need to ensure that each latent variable is properly labeled.
   - ❖ To name the latent variables, double click within the desired ellipse.
   - ❖ You will be presented with the **Object Properties** box, as seen below.
   - ❖ Click on the **Text** tab. In the **Variable name** box, type the desired name for the latent variable, and close the box by clicking on the **X** in the upper right-hand corner. Amos applies the change directly to the path diagram.

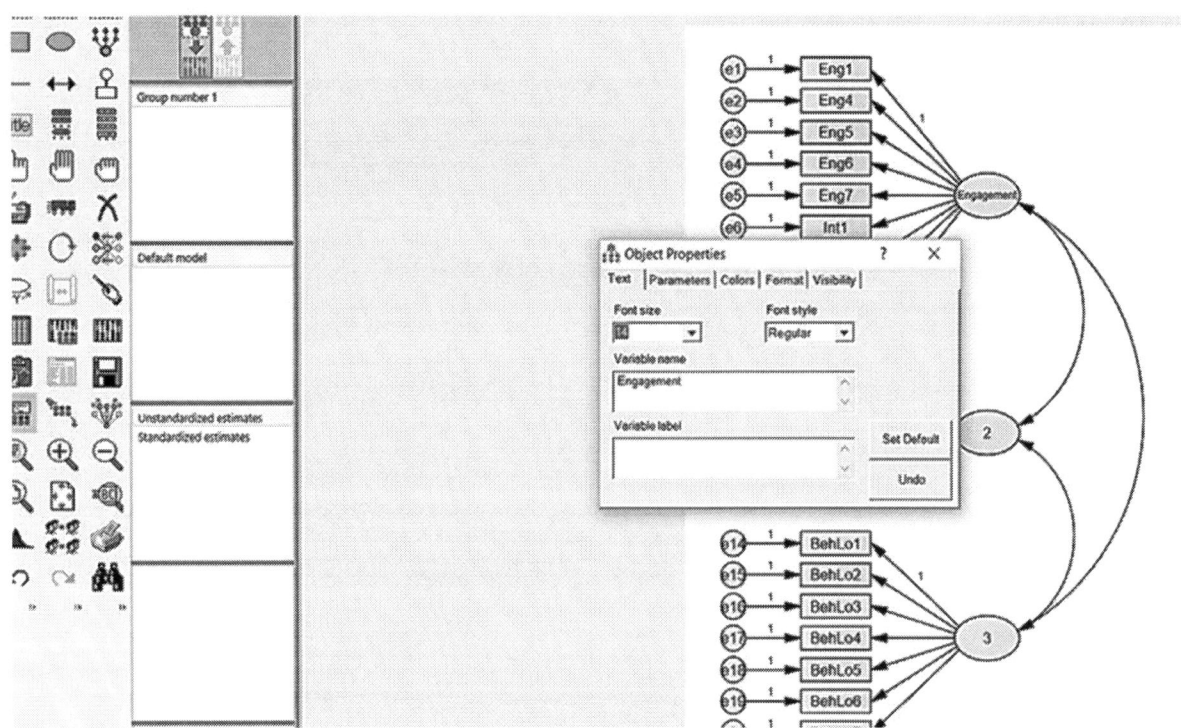

8. Model identification must be ensured next. Without introducing constraints in the model, the scales of the latent variables will be meaningless. Hence, one factor loading on each latent variable must be fixed to **1** (set as a marker variable). To achieve this:

   ❖ Double click on the desired arrow pointing to the observed variable.
   ❖ You will be presented with the **Object Properties** box, as seen below.
   ❖ Click on the **Parameters** tab and type **1** in the field labeled **Regression weight**, and close the box by clicking on the **X** in the upper right-hand corner. Amos applies the change directly to the path diagram.

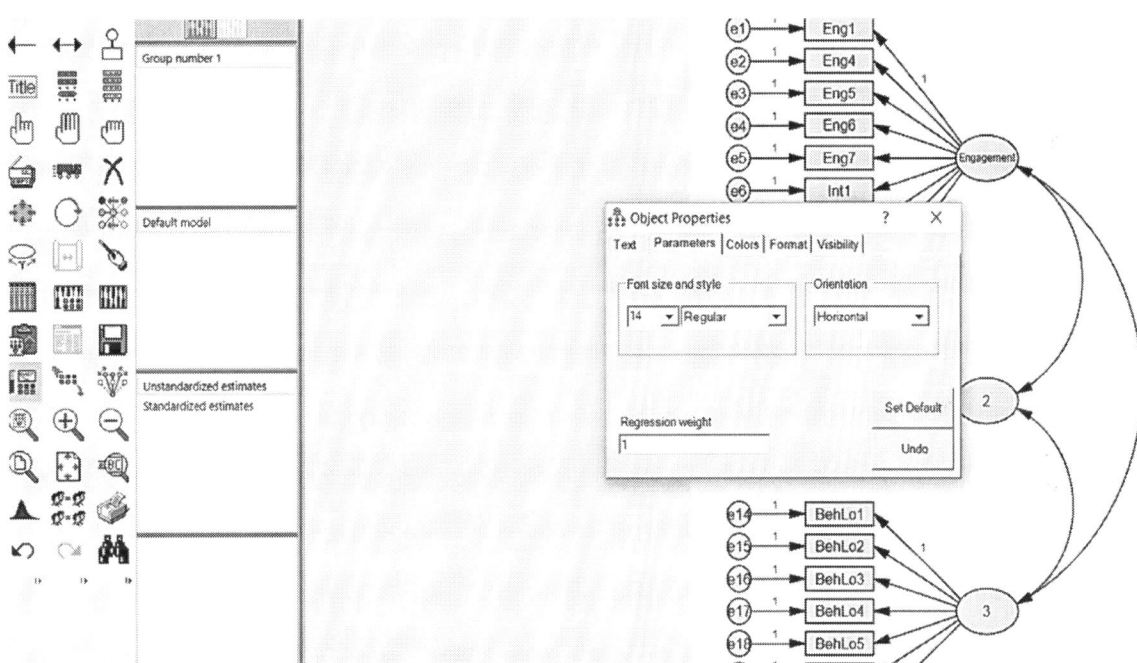

9. Objects on the interface can be moved by clicking on the **Move Objects** button on the tool bar, then click on the desired object and drag it to where you want it. Objects on the interface can also be deleted by clicking on the **Erase Objects** button on the tool bar, then click on the desired object to delete it, as seen below.

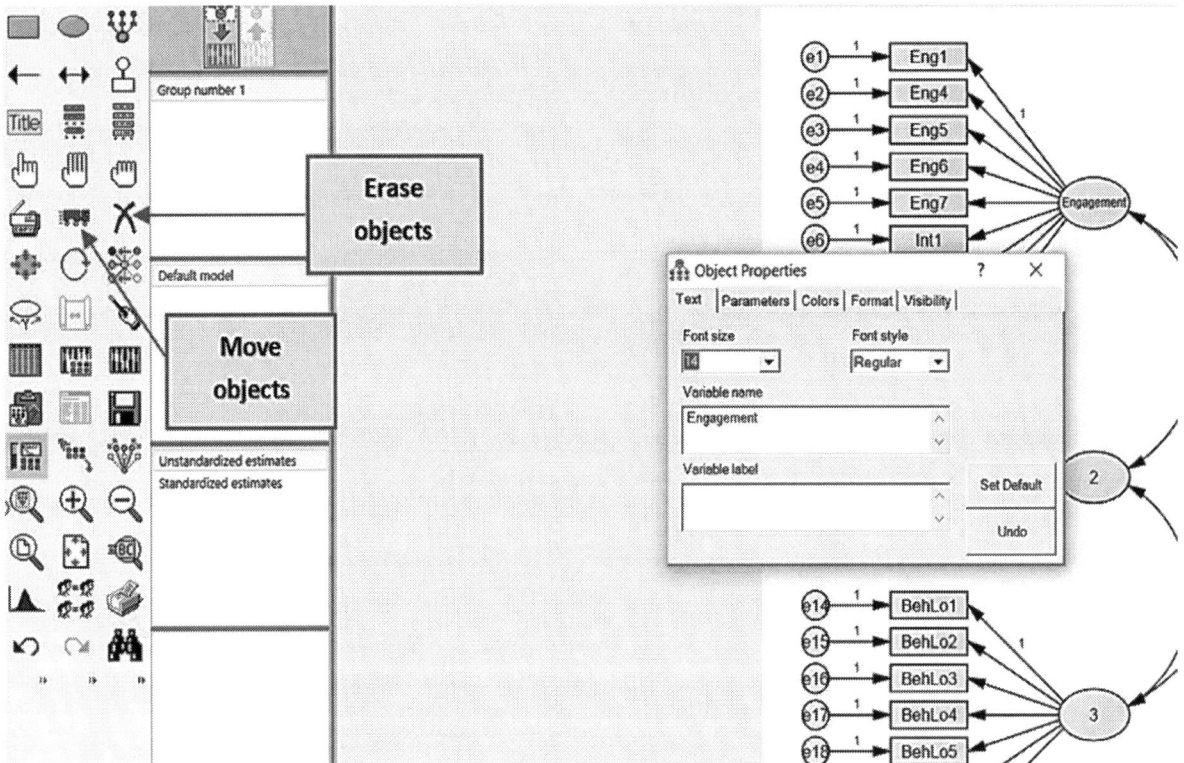

10. Before estimating the model, there is the need to specify the nature of output required. To achieve this:

- ❖ Click on the **Analysis properties** tab, you will be presented with the **Analysis Properties** box, as seen below.
- ❖ Click on the **Output** tab and choose the following options: **Minimization history**, **Standardized estimates**, **Squared multiple correlations**, **Modification indices**, **Correlations of estimates** and **Covariances of estimates**.
- ❖ Close the box by clicking on the **X** in the upper right-hand corner.

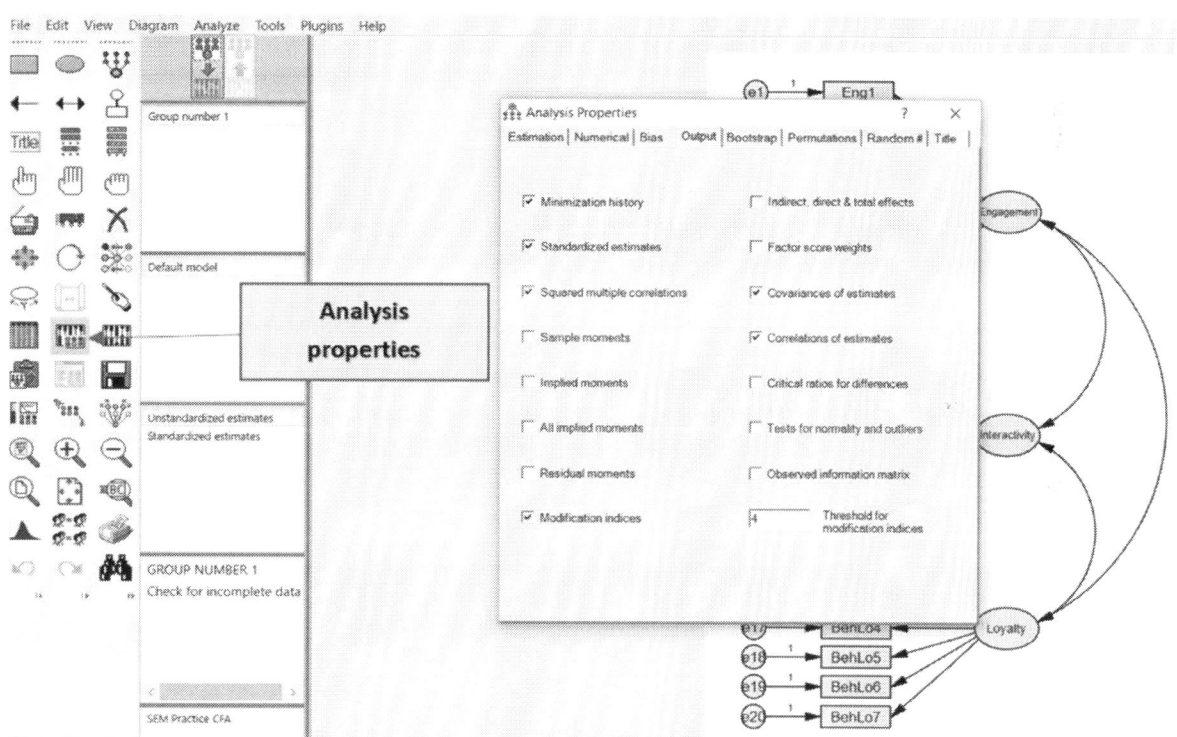

11. Save the Measurement model created by clicking on the **Save the current path diagram** tab. You will be presented with the **Save As** box, as seen below.

    ❖ Click in the **File name** box and type the desired name.
    ❖ Click **Save.**
    ❖ Now close the entire Amos interface, locate the CFA model that was just saved, in the folder in which it was saved and reopen it.

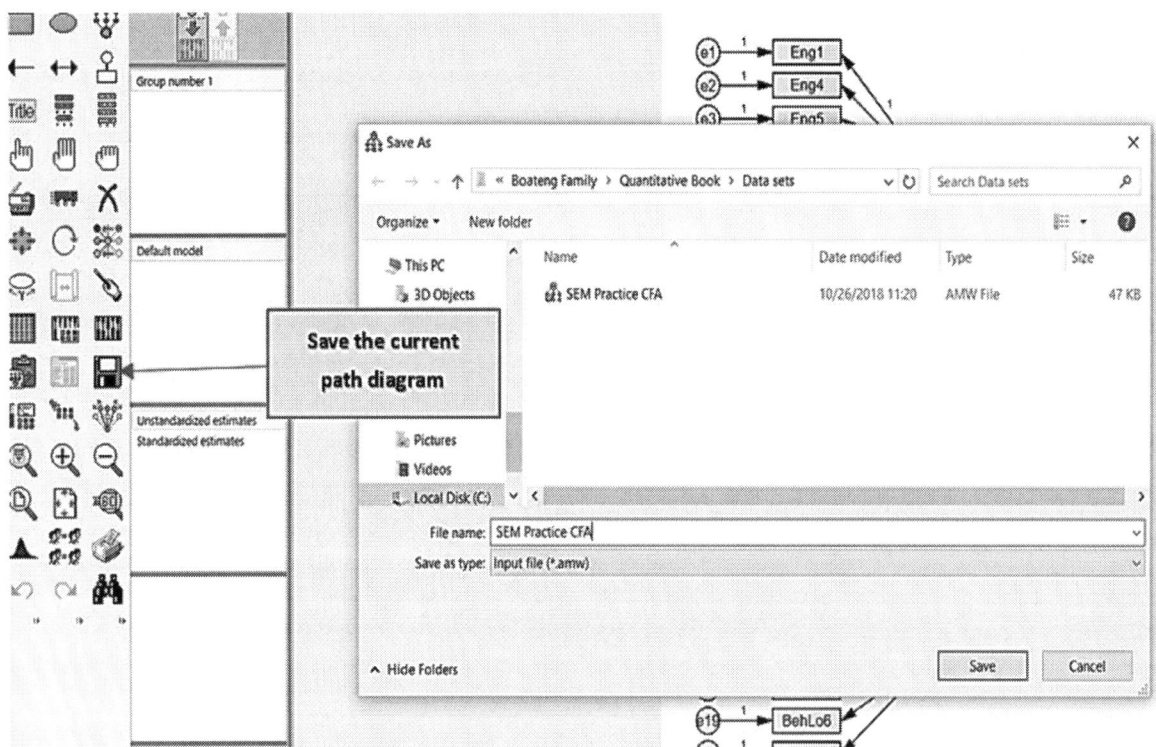

12. To run the CFA, click the **Calculate estimates** tab and view the graphical output by clicking the **View the output path diagram** tab. The tabular output can also be viewed by clicking the **View text** tab. You can also go back to view the original model without the estimates by clicking the **View the input path diagram** (model specification) tab, as seen below. The output is able to show both **Standardized** and **Unstandardized estimates** of which the researcher can select which one he or she would like to view.

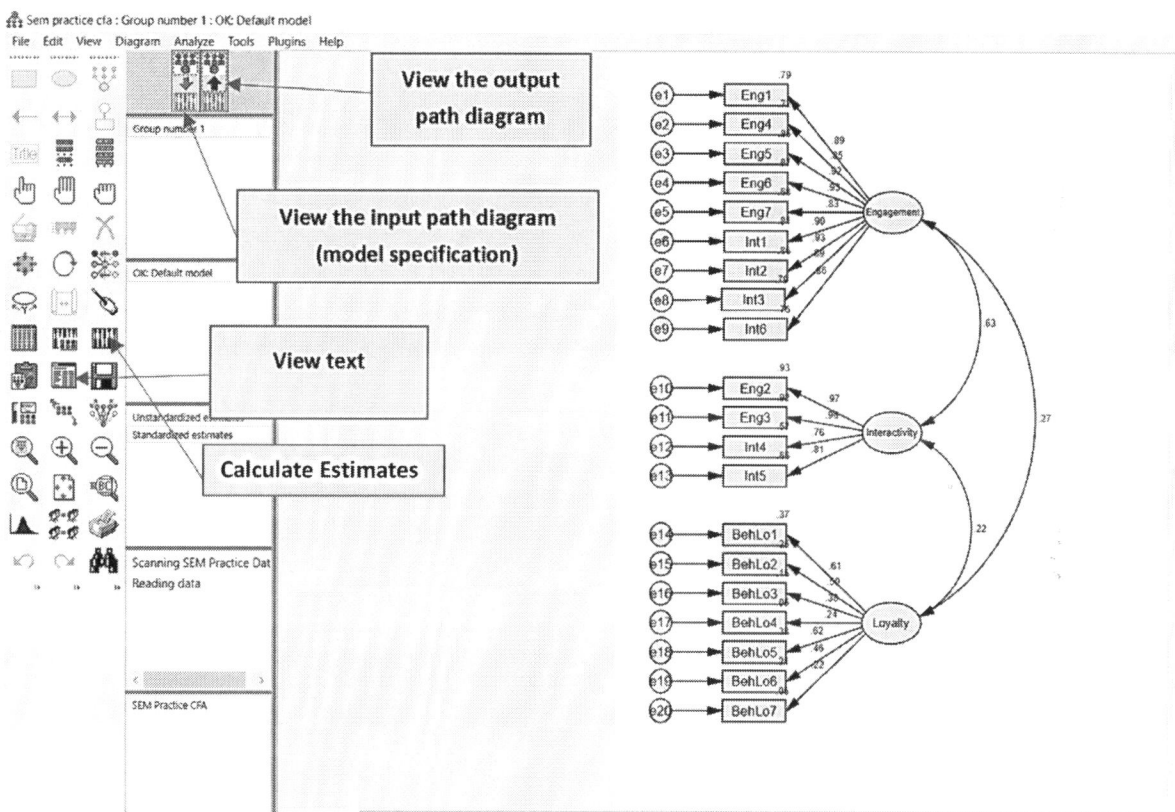

13. Upon clicking the **View text** tab, you will be presented with the **Amos Output** box where you can find the parameter **Estimates**, **Model fit** and **Modification indices** as seen in the image below, to enable you determine whether or not the model requires modification. You can click on either of them to obtain their full details.

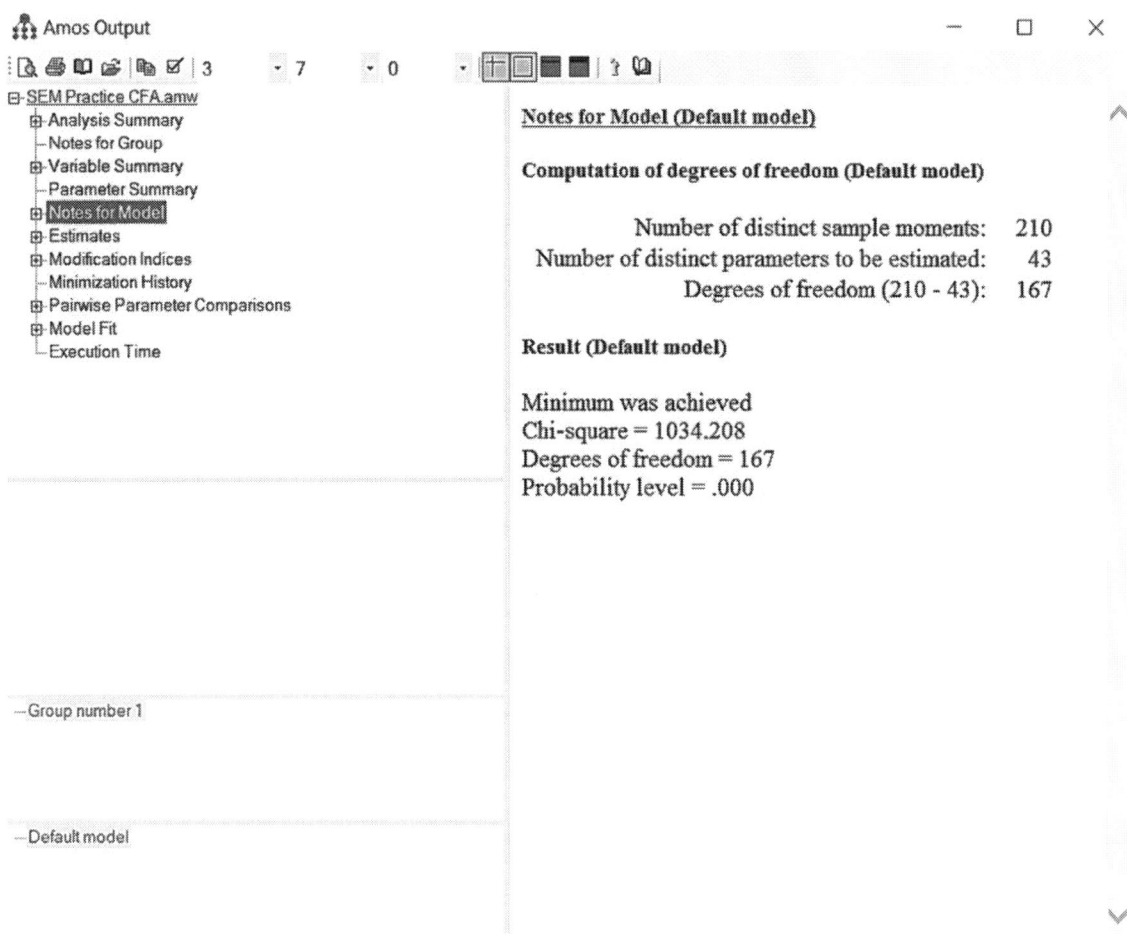

Analyzing Confirmatory Factor Analysis (CFA) Output

CFA output comes in both a standardized and an unstandardized form. However, it is the standardized loadings for each variable that are reported in the final loadings table. These **Standardized Estimates**, **Model fit** statistics, as well as the **reliability** and **validity** of the resulting measurement model must be checked to ensure that they all fall within the acceptable thresholds, and then reported as discussed in Chapters 6 and 7 above. In instances where the model does not meet any of the recommended criteria, the researcher is required to revise the model, by deleting some indicators utilizing the model modification indices as previously discussed to ensure that an adequate model is obtained.

Procedure for Stage 2 - Structural Stage using Amos

1. Open the previously saved CFA model that was created in the preceding section.
   - ❖ Click on **View** at the top right of the screen and select **Interface Properties.**
   - ❖ You will be presented with the **Interface Properties** window, as shown below.
   - ❖ Under the **Page Layout** tab, in the **Paper Size** box, select **Landscape - A4**.
   - ❖ Click **Apply**.
   - ❖ Close the box by clicking on the **X** in the upper right-hand corner.

   This will enable you to maximize the work space in order to create a path model.

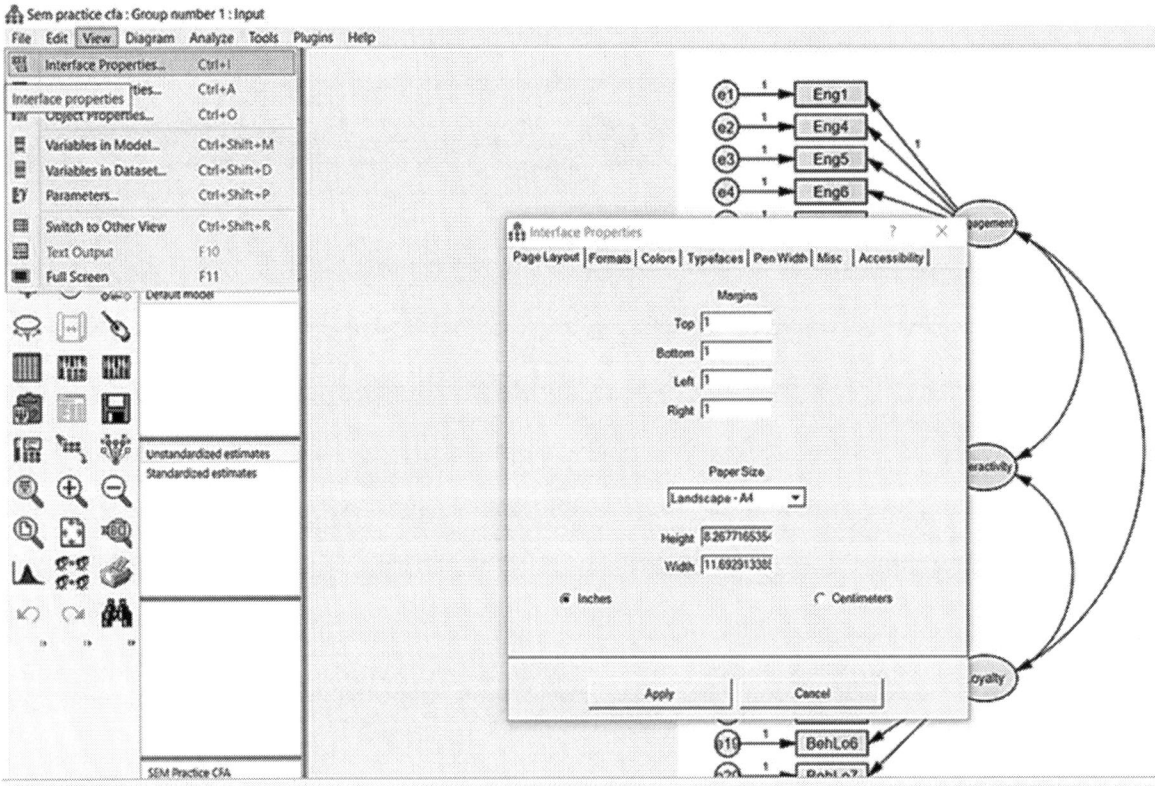

2. Create the path model by moving around the latent variables, as presented below.
   - ❖ First, delete the covariances linking the individual latent variables.
   - ❖ Using the **Select one object at a time** tab, select and move the latent variables. together with their observed variables and residuals to the desired positions.
   - ❖ With single headed arrows, indicate the positions of the endogenous and exogenous variables.
   - ❖ Using the **Deselect all objects** tab, deselect all the objects that were previously selected.
   - ❖ You can also use the **Rotate the indicators of a latent variable** tab to rotate the indicators to face a particular direction.

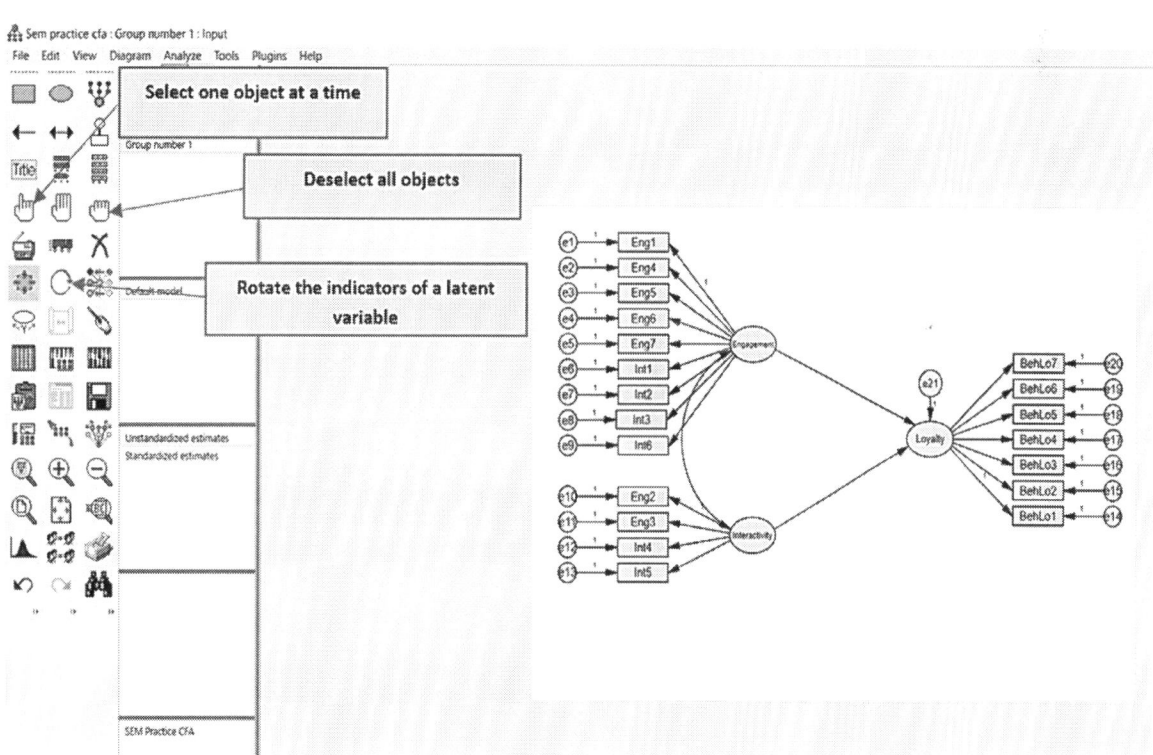

3. Save the path model as a new file, as is presented below.
    - ❖ Click on **File** at the top right of the screen and select **Save As...**
    - ❖ You will be presented with the **Save As** window.
    - ❖ Select the desired location in which to save the file.
    - ❖ Type the desired name of the file into the **File name** box.
    - ❖ Click **Save**.

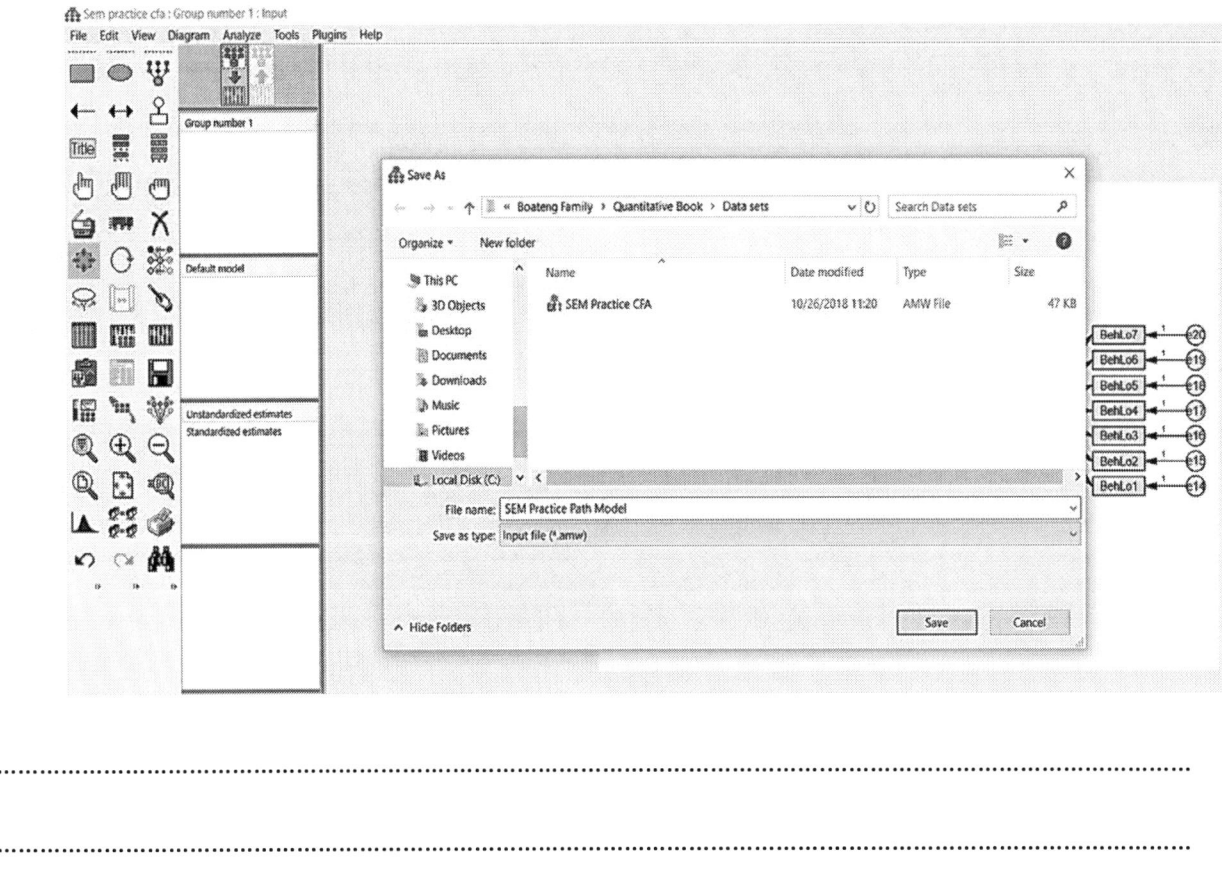

4. Now close the entire Amos interface, locate the path model that was just saved, in the folder in which it was saved and reopen it. Before estimating the model, there is the need to specify the nature of output required. To achieve this:

   ❖ Click on the **Analysis properties** tab, you will be presented with the **Analysis Properties** box, as seen below.

   ❖ Click on the **Output** tab and choose the following options: **Minimization history**, **Standardized estimates**, **Squared multiple correlations**, **Correlations of estimates** and **Covariances of estimates**.

   ❖ Close the box by clicking on the **X** in the upper right-hand corner.

   ❖ Click on the **Calculate Estimates** tab to run the path analysis, as shown below.

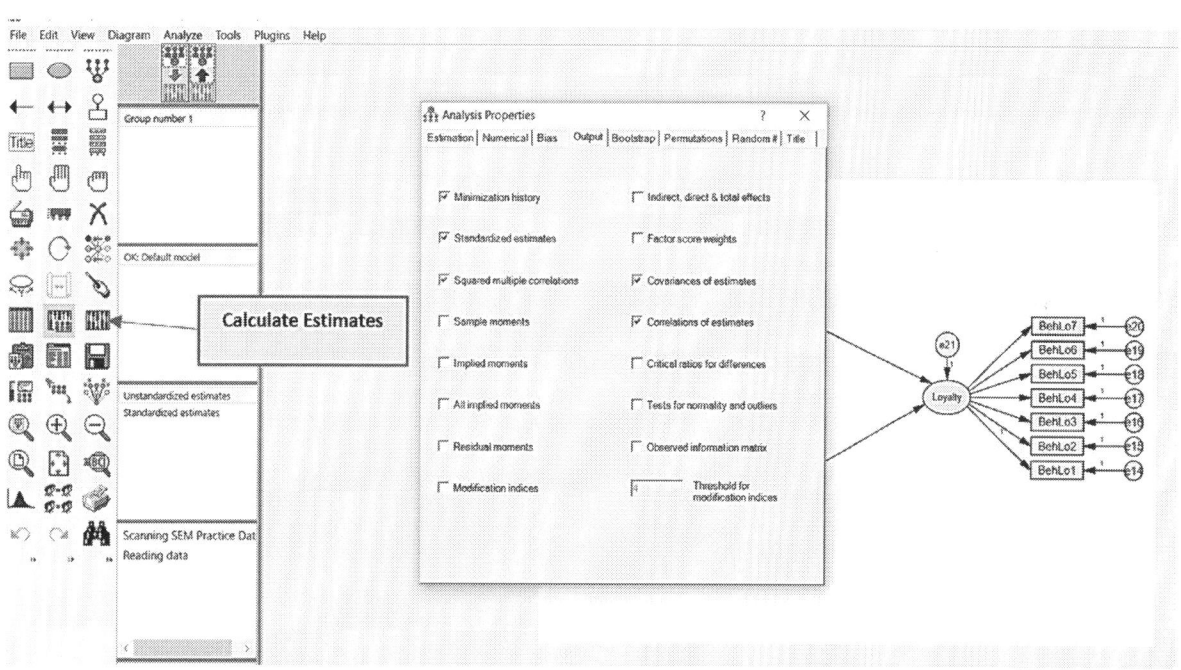

5. To view the graphical output, click the **View the output path diagram** tab. The tabular output can also be viewed, as seen below, by clicking the **View text** tab. Click **Estimates** to see the various parameter estimates. Here you will be able to view those paths that were significant and those that were not, along with their **R square** value(s), which tells us the amount of variance in the dependent variable that is explained by the model. The fit indices for the model are also presented here.

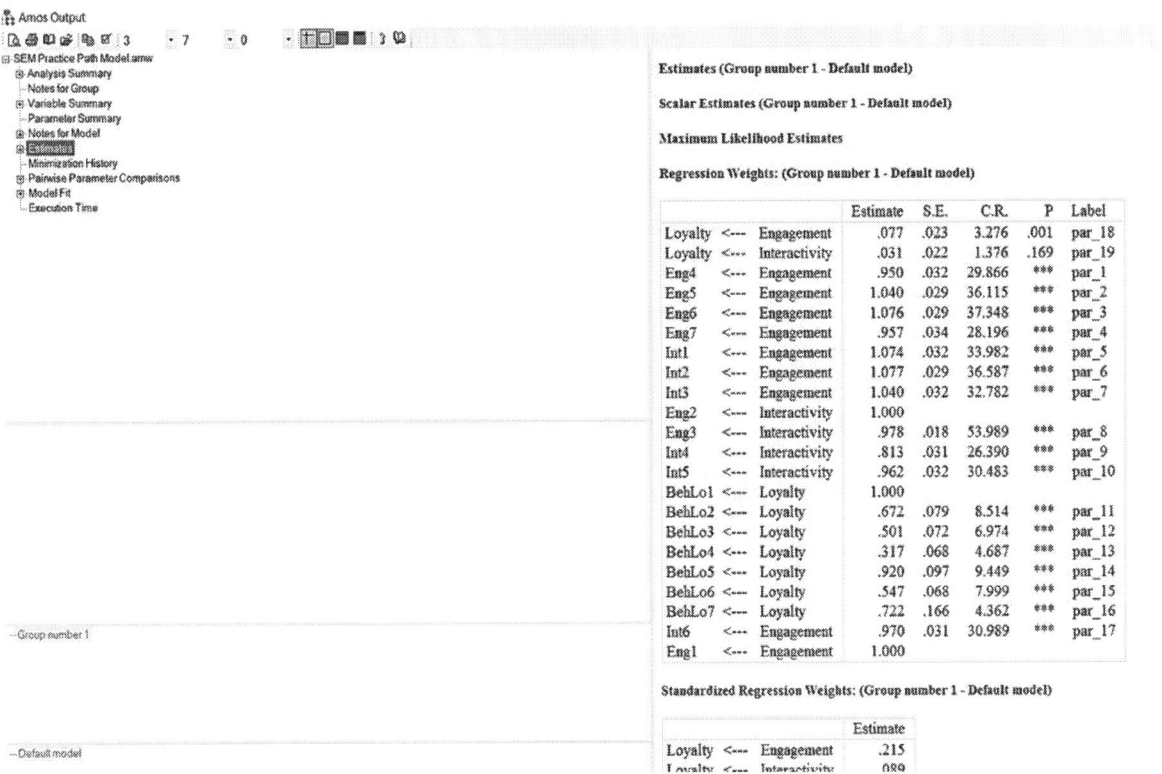

Analyzing Path Analysis (PA) Output

In analyzing the output from a path analysis, the aim of the researcher is to find support for or a lack thereof for their hypotheses. To achieve this several criteria must be satisfied. These criteria can be classified as global or local tests.[32] Hypotheses are deemed to be supported when the local test criteria are satisfied. However, for a local test to hold, all the global test criteria have to be satisfied. In order of importance, the global tests of **model fit** must first be met. This is because we cannot have confidence in a hypothesis with a **significant α level**, if the overall model has poor fit. The global test of the amount of variance explained (**R square**) is considered next. Regardless of obtaining a significant α level and a good model fit, if R square is very low, then the relationships being tested have no relevance given that they do not explain enough of the variance in the dependent variable.

Although all researchers would ideally like for all their hypotheses to be supported when running a path analysis, there are certain instances where the researcher ends up with some insignificant paths between the latent variables. In case this happens, there is a next level of analysis that can be conducted, especially for those researchers whose aim is to build a model to explain a particular phenomenon. Here the researcher tests a series of structural models, called **Nested models** in order to arrive at the best fitting model, which better explains the phenomenon under study.

Nested Models

A nested model, as used in this guide, is a model that utilizes the same latent variables as used in a previous path analysis, but specifies at least one less path to be estimated than the original baseline model. Here, at least one path at a time, usually the insignificant ones, is deleted in succession from the initially estimated path model. Each path or set of paths that is deleted forms a new alternative model, whose fit is compared with that of the original model (the baseline model). This is done consecutively until an alternative model is obtained whose fit is better than that obtained after the initial path analysis. All of these alternative models are called reduced models, which are nested within the more restricted original model, which is the baseline model.[70] Hence, the term **Nested models**. This approach of testing and comparing alternative models with a baseline model, was proffered by Anderson and Gerbing[65] to enable researcher obtain a more parsimonious final model that best explains the phenomenon of interest.

In analyzing nested models, the **Predictive fit indices** of the alternative and baseline models, namely the **Root Mean Square Error of Approximation (RMSEA)**, the **Chi-square (χ^2)** statistic and the **Degrees of Freedom (df)**, along with the changes that occur in them as each alternative model is predicted are compared. Similarly, the **Comparative fit indices**, including the **Comparative Fit Index (CFI), the Incremental Fit Index (IFI)** and the **Tucker-Lewis Index (TLI)** along with the changes that occur in them as each alternative model is predicted are also compared. Ultimately, the model with the best fit, which could very well be the baseline model, is chosen as the final model to explain the phenomenon under study.

An example of the output from an alternative model comparison is presented in Table 6 overleaf. These nested models were tested as part of a larger SEM analysis conducted for a thesis on the 'influence of online relationship marketing on activities customer loyalty'. The results of the analysis indicate that in comparing the five alternative models (Model 1-5) with the baseline model, Model 2 is the model that best explains the influence of online relationship marketing on customer loyalty. This is because among all the alternative models, the path deleted in Model 2 led to an insignificant **Chi-square (χ^2)** statistic (which is the ideal case) and a huge improvement in the model fit as compared with that of the baseline model (see Table 6 overleaf). Hence, the choice of Model 2 as the best fitting alternative model.

Table 6 - Alternative Model Comparison[13]

Model	χ^2	df	$\Delta\chi^2$	Δdf	χ^2/df	CFI	RMSEA
Baseline model	13.3	6	-	-	2.2	0.99	0.05
Model 1	14.8	7	$\Delta\chi^2$ (b, m1) = 1.5*	1	2.1	0.99	0.05
Model 2	13.6	7	$\Delta\chi^2$ (b, m2) = 0.3	1	1.9	0.99	0.05
Model 3	15.4	7	$\Delta\chi^2$ (b, m3) = 2.1*	1	2.2	0.99	0.05
Model 4	14.4	7	$\Delta\chi^2$ (b, m4) = 1.1*	1	2.1	0.99	0.05
Model 5	22.2	8	$\Delta\chi^2$ (b, m5) = 8.9**	2	2.8	0.98	0.05

*p < 0.05, **p < 0.01

Chapter Summary

In this chapter the two-step approach to SEM analysis proposed by Anderson and Gerbing was discussed. Among others, readers learned the characteristics of the measurement model and the structural models, as well as how to perform a Confirmatory Factor Analysis (CFA) and a Path Analysis (PA) to derive a measurement and a structural model. The process of conducting an alternative model comparison was also treated. Chapter 9 presents a practical demonstration of a complete SEM analysis in practice, as was utilized in a thesis researching the influence of online relationship marketing activities on customer loyalty.

Chapter 9

Practical Demonstration of Structural Equation Modelling (SEM) in a Thesis Format

OBJECTIVES

The chapter begins with a description of the preliminary data preparation activities and sample characteristics. Descriptive statistics and Exploratory Factor Analysis (EFA) results are also presented. Subsequently, the analysis and results of the Structural Equation Modelling (SEM) are shown and discussed.

Reference to the published thesis (as a book):

Boateng, S. L. (2018). *Online Relationship Marketing, What Works in Ghana.* Charleston, USA: Kindle Direct Publishing (an Amazon Company). ISBN-13: 978-1727453652: Available on Amazon: https://amzn.to/2QPBBMi

PRELIMINARY DATA PREPARATION

The survey instrument was distributed to 500 respondents in the regional capitals of three regions in Ghana, namely Greater Accra, Western and Ashanti region. Out of 500, 449 completed surveys were returned, representing a response rate of 89.8%. These responses were coded and entered into SPSS 20, following which the data was verified and screened for any form of error, missing data or outliers (i.e., using Box and Whisker plots and normal probability plot) (Kline, 2011). The screening process revealed that several of the responses had more than 5% missing data. Therefore, it was decided to delete the responses that had missing values in various sections; resulting in the deletion of a total of 20 cases. Thus, excluding missing and unusable data, the resulting sample included 429 respondents; giving an effective response rate of 85.8%. There was also no evidence of outliers.

Consequently, the distribution of the resulting data set was then tested for normality, since factor analysis and structural equation modelling are both purported to require variables that are normally distributed (Hair et al., 2006). As such using SPSS 20, the absolute values of skewness and kurtosis for each value was generated to check if the data meets the criteria for normality. An inspection of the skewness and kurtosis estimates showed that the values fell within the recommended levels (as close to zero as possible) (Pallant, 2011), thereby indicating univariate normality. The characteristics of the sample used in the study are outlined in the next section.

SAMPLE CHARACTERISTICS

The results presented in Table 9.1 show the differences in the demographics of the respondents based on gender, age, education level, average monthly income, educational level and online channels used. It is evident from the findings that the sample showed a higher number of male (272) respondents than female (157), representing percentages of 63.4% and 36.6%, respectively. Majority of the respondents fell within the ages of 31-40 years (42.4%), with a modal monthly income of less than GHS 5000, being earned by 92.8% of the respondents. In terms of educational level, Table 9.1 indicates that the highest percentages were for respondents with a Diploma/HND (34%), followed by those with a secondary level education (31.9%) and then tertiary- undergraduate (24%), tertiary – postgraduate (8.9%) and primary (1.2%). Furthermore, it can be observed from the table that emails (100%) are the main online channels used in communication between banks and their customers, in addition to websites (79%) and social media (Facebook/Twitter) (38.5%).

Also, majority of the respondents are shown to patronize mainly Barclays Bank (16.3%), a foreign bank headquartered in the United Kingdom operating within the Ghanaian banking industry. Although, this number is followed closely by the Fidelity bank (16.3%), which is an indigenous Ghanaian bank equally competing in the same industry. In all, the respondents operate with 8 banks. Descriptive statistics are presented in the next section, summarizing the general features of the data set.

TABLE 9.1 PROFILE OF RESPONDENTS

Demographic Profile	Number of Respondents (N = 429)	Valid Percentage (%)
Gender		
Male	272	63.4
Female	157	36.6
Age		
18-20	2	0.5
21-30	121	28.2
31-40	182	42.4
41-50	97	22.6
Above 50	27	6.3

Demographic Profile	Number of Respondents (N = 429)	Valid Percentage (%)
Educational Level		
Primary	5	1.2
Secondary	137	31.9
Tertiary-Undergraduate	103	24.0
Tertiary-Postgraduate	38	8.9
Diploma/ HND	146	34.0
Average Monthly Income		
Less than GHS 5,000	398	92.8
GHS 5,000-GHS 10,000	28	6.5
GHS 11,000-GHS 15,000	2	0.5
Above GHS 15,000	1	0.2
Online Channels Used		
Email	429	100
Website	339	79
Social Media (Facebook/ Twitter)	165	38.5
Name of Bank		
Access Bank	35	8.2
Barclays Bank	70	16.3
Cal Bank	30	7.0
Ecobank	50	11.7
Fidelity Bank	70	16.3
Guaranty Trust Bank	64	14.9
Standard Chartered Bank	56	13.0
Zenith Bank	54	12.6

DESCRIPTIVE STATISTICS

Descriptive statistics are concise descriptive coefficients that help to describe and understand the characteristics of a data set, by providing brief summaries on the sample and the measures of the data. Pallant (2011) proffers that before performing any quantitative statistical analyses such as an Analysis of Variance (ANOVA), EFA or CFA, there is the need to obtain descriptive statistics for each of the variables. These may include measures of central tendency such as the mean, median and mode, as well as measures of dispersion including the standard deviation and the skewness and kurtosis. Table 9.2 shows the construct measures and descriptive statistics of the variables used in the data analysis.

These measures evaluate the degree to which the respondents agreed or disagreed with the statements in the survey instrument and show how each statement performed. The 30 variables displayed represent the measurement items of the five main constructs portrayed in the resulting framework for the study; Engagement (**Enga**), Interactivity (**Intera**), Calculative Commitment (**CalCom**), Online Trust (**OnTr**) and Customer Loyalty (**CuLo**).

TABLE 9.2 CONSTRUCT MEASURES AND DESCRIPTIVE STATISTICS

Scale Item	Variable Code	Mean	Standard Deviation	S.E. Mean
Interactivity				
My bank's website has a section for Frequently Asked Questions (FAQs)	**Intera1**	3.22	1.28	0.06
My bank has site navigation tools on their website	**Intera2**	3.42	1.25	0.06
My bank's website has a search tool that enables me to locate items	**Intera3**	3.60	1.29	0.06
I get the desired answers to my online enquiries	**Intera4**	3.62	1.32	0.06
24-hour live chat/help is available on my bank's website	**Intera5**	3.26	1.28	0.06

Scale Item	Variable Code	Mean	Standard Deviation	S.E. Mean
My bank promptly responds to my enquiries through email	Intera6	3.73	1.21	0.06
My bank's online platforms provide mechanisms that help me to evaluate and select appropriate products and services	Intera7	3.60	1.22	0.06
My bank offers exclusive webpages and information for customers on their website	Intera8	3.45	1.29	0.06
Engagement				
I write comments and messages on my bank's Facebook page	Enga1	2.40	1.22	0.06
I 'like' content posted on my bank's Facebook page	Enga2	2.50	1.36	0.07
I retweet comments posted on my bank's Twitter handle	Enga3	2.10	1.26	0.06
My bank's website has hotlinks to their Twitter/Facebook pages	Enga4	2.65	1.29	0.06
Other customers provide helpful information on my bank's Facebook page	Enga5	2.85	1.43	0.07
Calculative Commitment				
The management of my personal finances would be disrupted if I decided to stop patronizing my bank's services	CalCom1	3.66	0.81	0.04
I think that the cost in time, money and effort to switch to another bank is high	CalCom2	3.42	1.10	0.05
I am afraid something will be lost if I stop using my bank	CalCom3	3.28	1.20	0.06
Some aspects of my life will be affected if I cease patronising my bank	CalCom4	3.47	1.03	0.05
There are no banking services comparable to those offered by my bank	CalCom5	3.80	1.00	0.05
Online Trust				
I can count on my bank to ensure that transactions carried out on its website are without error	OnTr1	4.03	0.98	0.05

Scale Item	Variable Code	Mean	Standard Deviation	S.E. Mean
I think that the information presented on my bank's website is reliable	OnTr2	4.04	1.02	0.05
My bank keeps customers' best interests in mind	OnTr3	4.28	0.68	0.03
My bank makes every effort to address and solve customer concerns and problems online	OnTr4	4.06	0.83	0.04
I think that my bank would not do anything intentional on their website that would be unfair to customers	OnTr5	3.95	1.00	0.05
I feel like my privacy is protected while transacting with my bank online.	OnTr6	4.23	0.74	0.04
Customer Loyalty				
I will recommend my bank to anyone who seeks banking advice	CuLo1	4.13	0.61	0.03
I would be willing to pay a higher price for my bank's services over other banks	CuLo2	3.75	1.04	0.05
I prefer my bank to its competitors	CuLo3	4.14	0.67	0.03
My bank is the best bank for me	CuLo4	4.11	0.71	0.03
I would be willing to defend my bank in the face of any controversy	CuLo5	3.86	0.97	0.05
I would consider my bank as my first choice for patronizing banking services	CuLo6	4.05	0.70	0.03

As observed in the table, the statement '*My bank keeps customers' best interests in mind*' had the highest mean of 4.28. Whereas, the lowest mean of 2.10 was recorded on the statement '*I retweet comments posted on my bank's Twitter handle*'. This indicates that few of the respondents retweet comments posted on their bank's Twitter handle; assuming they follow their bank on twitter at all, since only 38.5% of them interact with their bank through social media (Facebook/Twitter). The coming section outlines the details of the Exploratory Factor Analysis (EFA) performed on the data set.

EXPLORATORY FACTOR ANALYSIS (EFA)

Prior to performing the EFA, the data set was subjected to some data screening procedures including checking for unengaged responses, as well as skewness and kurtosis to ascertain its suitability for factor analysis. After passing all the initial screening tests, 30 items in total were derived and used for the latent measures of the conceptual constructs. These were factor analysed using the Maximum Likelihood extraction method in SPSS version 20. An inspection of the correlation matrix revealed the presence of several coefficients of 0.4 and above. The Kaiser-Meyer-Olkin (KMO) value was 0.95, which exceeded the recommended value of 0.6 (Kaiser, 1970) and the Bartlett's Test of Sphericity reached statistical significance at p = 0.00 (Bartlett, 1954), thereby supporting the factorability of the correlation matrix. The results of the KMO and Bartlett's Test are depicted below in Table 9.3.

TABLE 9.3 KMO AND BARTLETT'S TEST

Kaiser-Meyer-Olkin Measure of Sampling Adequacy		0.947
Bartlett's Test of Sphericity	Approx. Chi-Square	10018.495
	df	435
	Sig.	0.000

Furthermore, the maximum likelihood extraction revealed the occurrence of five factors with eigenvalues greater than 1. The five-factor solution altogether explained a total of 64.43% of the variance, with the highest factor contributing 37.5% and the lowest factor contributing 2.2% respectively.

Rotation and Reliability of the EFA

To aid in the interpretation of these five factors, an Oblique (Promax) rotation was performed on the variables with Kaiser Normalisation, to determine which variables loaded on which factors. The rotated solution revealed the presence of a simple structure (Pallant, 2011), with all variables showing strong loadings and loading substantially on only one of the five factors. Although factor loadings of 0.3 to 0.4 are minimally acceptable, Hair *et al.* (2006) recommend that values greater that 0.5 be generally considered. Hence, variables that failed to meet the recommended criteria were excluded from subsequent analyses. In total 47 items were deleted and excluded from further analysis.

In addition, the internal reliabilities of the constructs were assessed. Reliability of a scale indicates how free the *scale* is from random error and thus exhibits internal consistency. As such, Pallant (2011) proposes that the reliability of scales used in a data analysis must be assessed to ensure that the individual items which come together to form a factor, are all measuring the same attribute. The most common indicator used to check for internal consistency is the Cronbach's alpha (α) coefficient, which was used to check the reliability of the five factors generated through the EFA. Krabbe (2017) opines that ideally the value for the Cronbach's alpha (α) coefficient should fall between 0.7 and 0.9 for it to be reliable. Also, to test the significance of the variables that loaded onto the factors, item-to total correlation was set above 0.3 (Tabachnick & Fidell, 2007).

Table 9.4 overleaf depicts measurement properties from the Maximum Likelihood extraction and Promax rotation of the final variables retained after the EFA, as well as the internal consistency measures (Cronbach's alpha (α), Item-total correlation and α if item is deleted) of the various items.

Table 9.4 Rotated Factor Matrix and Internal Consistencies

Item	Variables	Loading	Variance explained	Cronbach's alpha (α)	Item-total correlation	α if item is deleted
Factor 1	Intera1	.75	80.31	0.96	.80	.95
	Intera2	.94			.87	.95
	Intera3	1.01			.89	.95
	Intera4	.75			.89	.95
	Intera5	.87			.83	.95
	Intera6	.50			.74	.96
	Intera7	.82			.87	.95
	Intera8	.85			.85	.95
Factor 2	Enga1	.85	32.9	0.92	.84	.90
	Enga2	1.00			.89	.88
	Enga3	.64			.70	.92
	Enga4	.70			.80	.90
	Enga5	.67			.76	.91
Factor 3	CalCom1	.53	18.08	0.88	.68	.87
	CalCom2	.92			.68	.86
	CalCom3	.78			.79	.84

Item	Variables	Loading	Variance explained	Cronbach's alpha (α)	Item-total correlation	α if item is deleted
	CalCom4	.77			.755	.84
	CalCom5	.54			.698	.86
Factor 4	OnTr1	.72	16.8	0.86	.72	.83
	OnTr2	.63			.669	.84
	OnTr3	.50			.57	.86
	OnTr4	.54			.67	.84
	OnTr5	.85			.76	.82
	OnTr6	.50			.58	.85
Factor 5	CuLo1	.67	13.2	0.85	.51	.85
	CuLo2	.53			.61	.84
	CuLo3	.67			.65	.82
	CuLo4	.80			.70	.82
	CuLo5	.87			.73	.81
	CuLo6	.73			.69	.82

Extraction Method: Maximum Likelihood. **Rotation Method:** Promax

The table shows the variables that were eventually retained after the EFA was performed on the data set. It is worthy to note that during the process of appraisal, a strong theoretical rationale was maintained while selecting the final measurement items for further analysis. Thus, the final scales used to measure Engagement, Interactivity, Calculative Commitment, Online Trust and

Customer Loyalty were carefully appraised based on their measurement properties (loadings and variance explained) and their internal consistencies using Cronbach's alpha (α), Item-total correlation and α if item is deleted. Subsequently, an assessment of Common Method Variance (CMV) was conducted on the data set. This is further discussed in the next section.

ASSESSMENT OF COMMON METHOD VARIANCE (CMV)

As observed from Table 9.4 above, Factor 1 exhibited a high level of variance explained, thus eliciting some concern about potential problems associated with common method variance. Common Method Variance (CMV) refers to the erroneous variance in statistical analysis that can be attributed to the method of measurement, rather than to the constructs that the measurement items are purported to represent (Chang, van Witteloostuijn & Eden, 2010). This may lead to a systematic measurement error, causing bias in the estimates of the true relationships among the theoretical constructs. For that reason, Harman's one-factor test was used as part of the analysis to empirically test for any potential issue of common method variance. The main assumption of this test is that if a significant amount of CMV exists, one general factor will account for majority of the total variance among the variables (Fuller *et al.*, 2016; Park, Lee & Kim, 2014; Podsakoff & Organ, 1986). To perform this test, all the 30 measurement items of the predictor variables were entered into an exploratory factor analysis, using unrotated maximum likelihood estimation, and extracting only one factor. Harman's one-factor test reveals bias when more than 50% variance is extracted in the single factor (Fuller *et al.*, 2016). In this case, the single merged factor accounted for less than 50% of the variance (36.6%), which indicates that CMV does not pose a major concern and is therefore unlikely to affect the interpretation of the results (Lonial & Carter, 2015; Orgambídez-Ramos & Borrego-Alés, 2014; Jansen, Van Den Bosch & Volberda, 2005). The post-study framework resulting from the preliminary data analysis discussed above is explained in the ensuing section.

POST-STUDY FRAMEWORK

As depicted in Table 9.4, some elements captured in the proposed conceptual framework fell through during the exploratory factor analysis (EFA); namely Personalization, Collaboration, Affective Commitment and Normative Commitment. Thus, the proposed conceptual framework with its identified constructs and postulated hypotheses, as presented earlier (see reference book) was modified to reflect these new developments. This resulted in a revised framework that better models the nature of the ORM activities of Ghanaian banks and their impact on the mediating and outcome variables. The revised framework as shown in Figure 9.1, delineates two main ORM activities practiced by Ghanaian banks, namely Engagement and Interactivity. Also, out of the three dimensions of customer commitment, Calculative commitment emerged as the main form of commitment exhibited by Ghanaian customers towards their banks. Thereby, culminating in 11 revised hypotheses to be tested, as observed in Figure 9.1. This post-study framework was subsequently used in conducting the Structural Equation Modelling (SEM) part of the data analysis, which is discussed into detail in the ensuing section.

ANALYSIS AND RESULTS OF STRUCTURAL EQUATION MODELLING

As discussed in the preceding chapter, Structural Equation Modelling (SEM) was used to test the hypotheses proposed in the research model. The two-stage approach to SEM recommended by Anderson and Gerbing (1988) was adopted in performing the SEM analysis; the rationale for which is discussed in the same chapter.

In **Stage 1 - Measurement phase**, the causal relationships between the observed variables, also referred to as the measurement items and the underlying theoretical constructs were specified. This was done by conducting a confirmatory factor analysis, resulting in the generation of a measurement model using Amos 22. Following from Stage 1, the paths or causal relationships between the dependent and independent variables were evaluated by means of a structural model in **Stage 2 – Structural phase.** The mode of the analysis conducted, as well as the results from the two stages are presented and discussed in the successive sections.

FIGURE 9.1 POST-STUDY FRAMEWORK

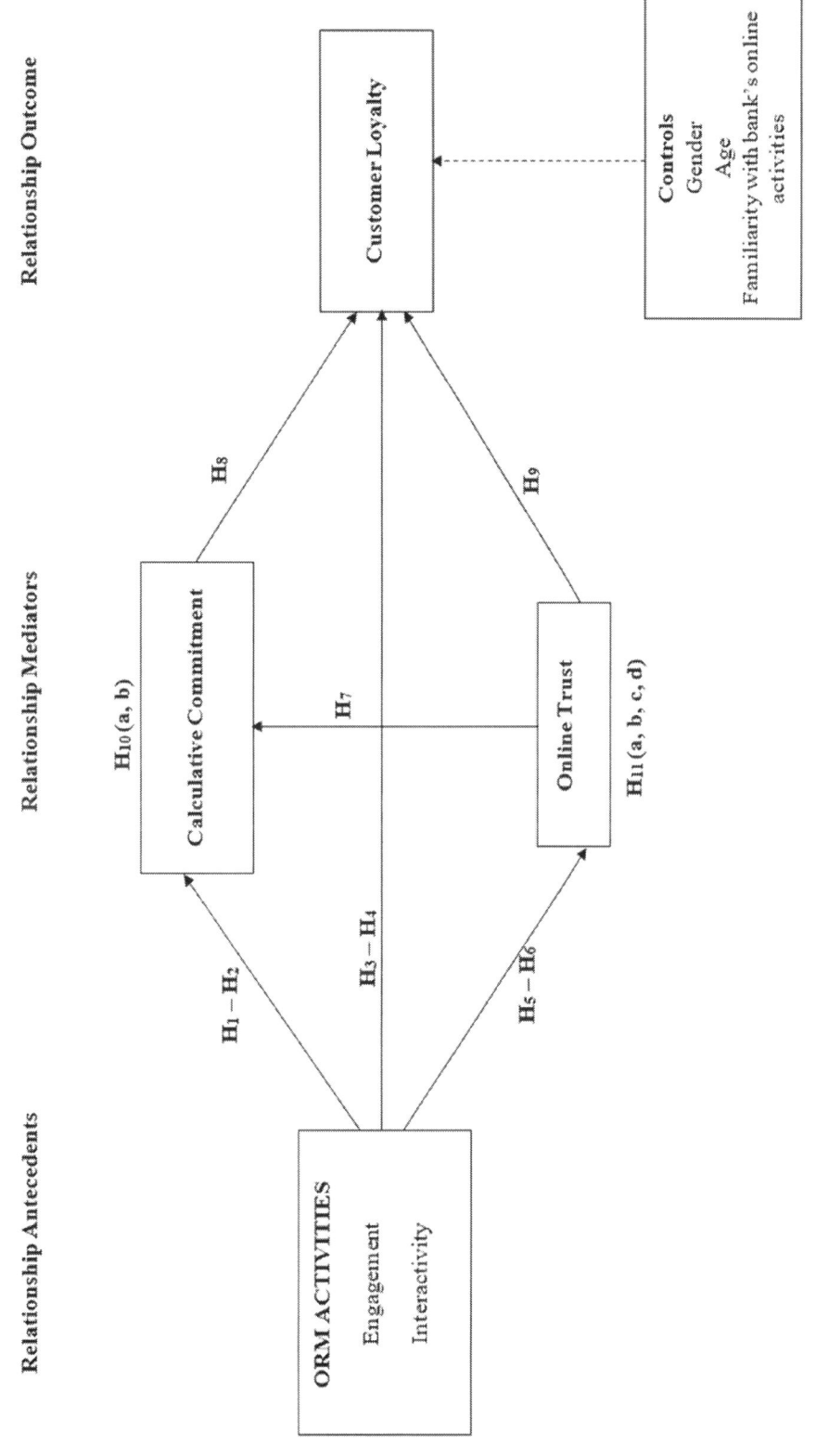

Stage 1 - Measurement Phase

At this stage, the regression structure among the latent variables is specified (Byrne, 2010). This was done by means of a CFA where the unidimensionality and internal consistency, as well as the reliability and validity of each variable was assessed. The CFA was used to test whether the data collected was consistent with the research model earlier specified (Prebensen, Woo, Chen & Uysal, 2012). Thus, the overall fit of the measurement model with a total of five constructs and thirty observed variables was tested using confirmatory factor analysis. Although all the standardized parameter estimates for each variable were all significant at p < 0.001, the fit indices of the initial measurement model indicated that the model needed to be respecified. Some of the indices were not at the required levels of acceptance (Schreiber, 2008). For example, the Root Mean Square Error of Approximation (RMSEA) = 0.07; even though χ^2 (Chi-square) = 1112.6, df (degrees of freedom) = 395 and χ^2/df ratio = 2.8. Also, the Comparative Fit Index (CFI) = 0.93, Incremental Fit Index (IFI) = 0.93 and Tucker-Lewis Index (TLI) = 0.92. Whereas, Standardised Root Mean Square Residual (SRMR) = 0.06. These indices are summarised in Table 9.5.

TABLE 9.5 FIT INDICES FOR MEASUREMENT MODEL

Fit Indices	Criteria	Initial level	Adjusted level
χ^2 (Chi-square)/df (degrees of freedom)	≤ 2 or 3	2.80	2.2
Comparative fit index (CFI)	≥ 0.95	0.93	0.97
Incremental fit index (IFI)	≥ 0.95	0.93	0.97
Tucker-Lewis index (TLI)	≥ 0.95	0.92	0.96
Root Mean Square Error of Approximation (RMSEA)	≤ 0.06 to 0.08	0.07	0.05
Standardised Root Mean Square Residual (SRMR)	≤ 0.08	0.06	0.04

Sources: Schreiber (2008); Schreiber *et al.* (2006)

Hence, the model was adjusted to improve the fit indices and obtain a better model fit. Some redundant items were deleted from selected variables, based on the model modification indices provided in the initial analysis. A total of seven items were removed prior to further analysis in a bid to enhance the fit of the measurement model. The details of the measurement items, their codes and those items that were deleted are shown in Table 9.6.

TABLE 9.6 MEASUREMENT MODEL ITEMS AND THEIR DESCRIPTION

Original Item	Item Code	Item Deleted
Interactivity		
My bank's website has a section for Frequently Asked Questions (FAQs)	Intera1	**Deleted**
My bank has site navigation tools on their website	Intera2	
My bank's website has a search tool that enables me to locate items	Intera3	
I get the desired answers to my online enquiries	Intera4	
24-hour live chat/ help is available on my bank's website	Intera5	
My bank promptly responds to my enquiries through email	Intera6	**Deleted**
My bank's online platforms provide mechanisms that help me to evaluate and select appropriate products and services	Intera7	
My bank offers exclusive webpages and information for customers on their website	Intera8	
Engagement		
I write comments and messages on my bank's Facebook page	Enga1	
I 'like' content posted on my bank's Facebook page	Enga2	

Original Item	Item Code	Item Deleted
I retweet comments posted on my bank's Twitter handle	Enga3	**Deleted**
My bank's website has hotlinks to their Twitter/ Facebook pages	Enga4	
Other customers provide helpful information on my bank's Facebook page	Enga5	
Calculative Commitment		
The management of my personal finances would be disrupted if I decided to stop patronizing my bank's services	CalCom1	**Deleted**
I think that the cost in time, money and effort to switch to another bank is high	CalCom2	
I am afraid something will be lost if I stop using my bank	CalCom3	
Some aspects of my life will be affected if I cease patronising my bank	CalCom4	
There are no banking services comparable to those offered by my bank	CalCom5	
Online Trust		
I can count on my bank to ensure that transactions carried out on its website are without error	OnTr1	
I think that the information presented on my bank's website is reliable	OnTr2	**Deleted**
My bank keeps customers' best interests in mind	OnTr3	
My bank makes every effort to address and solve customer concerns and problems online	OnTr4	
I think that my bank would not do anything intentional on their website that would be unfair to customers	OnTr5	

Original Item	Item Code	Item Deleted
I feel like my privacy is protected while transacting with my bank online.	OnTr6	**Deleted**
Customer Loyalty		
I will recommend my bank to anyone who seeks banking advice	CuLo1	**Deleted**
I would be willing to pay a higher price for my bank's services over other banks	CuLo2	
I prefer my bank to its competitors	CuLo3	
My bank is the best bank for me	CuLo4	
I would be willing to defend my bank in the face of any controversy	CuLo5	
I would consider my bank as my first choice for patronizing banking services	CuLo6	

Following the deletions, CFA was once again performed, without the seven deleted items listed above. The goodness-of-fit indices were significantly improved, with individual indices meeting the required criteria for acceptance (Schreiber, 2008). χ^2 (Chi-square) = 473.2, df (degrees of freedom) = 220 and χ^2/df ratio = 2.2. Comparative Fit Index (CFI) = 0.97, Incremental Fit Index (IFI) = 0.97 and Tucker-Lewis Index (TLI) = 0.96; Root Mean Square Error of Approximation (RMSEA) = 0.05 and Standardised Root Mean Square Residual (SRMR) = 0.04 (see Table 9.6). Chi-square is generally sensitive to large sample sizes (Hair *et al.*, 2010), so although the chi-square was still significant at $p = 0.00$, the values of the remaining indices presuppose that the model sufficiently fits with the data. Thus, there was no need for additional adjustments to be made to the model. The resulting final measurement model is presented in Figure 9.2.

FIGURE 9.2 FINAL CFA MEASUREMENT MODEL

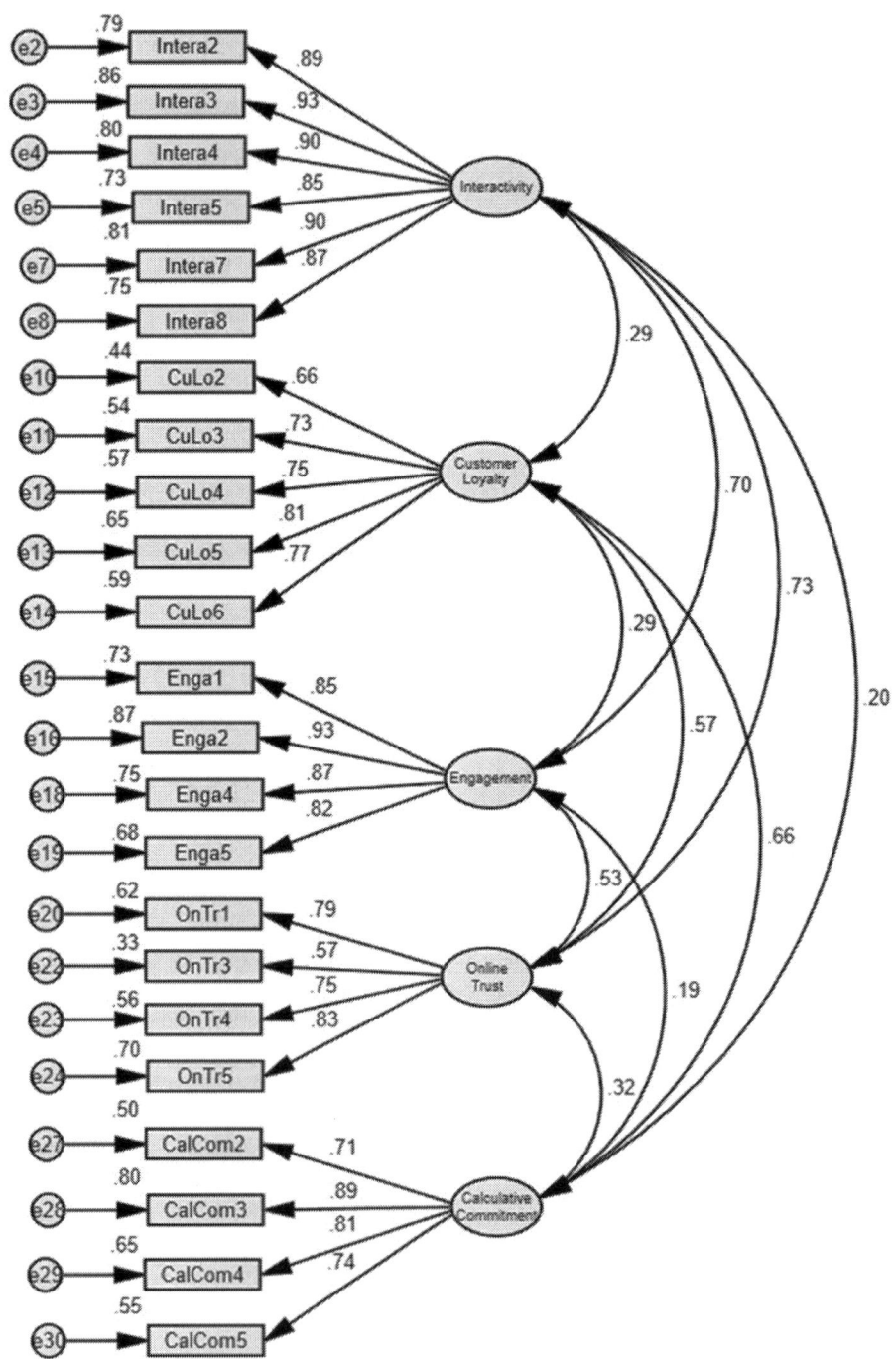

χ^2 (Chi-square) = 473.2, *df* (degrees of freedom) = 220, p = 0.00, χ^2/df = 2.2, RMSEA = 0.05

Validity and Reliability of Final Measurement Model

Reliability

Reliability for the constructs was first assessed using Cronbach's alpha (α) ≥ 0.7, and subsequently using the confirmatory factor analysis. Table 9.7 shows the overall CFA results for the final measurement model (see Figure 9.1). The table shows that the factor loadings for each item are significantly high, ranging from 0.57 to 0.93. Hair *et al.* (2006) recommends that factor loadings of 0.5 or more are required for an item to be reliable. The Cronbach's alpha (α) for each construct also exceeded the suggested level of 0.7 (Krabbe, 2017). Additionally, from the CFA, the CR and AVE values for each construct exceeded the recommended thresholds of CR ≥ 0.6 and AVE ≥ 0.5 (Bagozzi & Yi, 2012; Awwad & Agti, 2011). Thus, it can be concluded that the measurement model specified is a reliable fit with the data gathering for this research.

TABLE 9.7 CFA RESULTS FOR FINAL MEASUREMENT MODEL

Construct	Item code	Factor Loading	t value	R^2 value	CR	AVE	α
Interactivity	Intera2	0.89***	Fixed	0.80	**0.96**	**0.79**	**0.96**
	Intera3	0.93***	30.95	0.86			
	Intera4	0.90***	28.43	0.80			
	Intera5	0.85***	25.29	0.73			
	Intera7	0.90***	28.71	0.81			
	Intera8	0.87***	26.22	0.75			
Engagement	Enga1	0.86***	Fixed	0.73	**0.93**	**0.76**	**0.92**
	Enga2	0.93***	26.57	0.87			
	Enga4	0.87***	23.48	0.75			
	Enga5	0.82***	21.52	0.68			
Calculative Commitment	CalCom2	0.71***	Fixed	0.50	**0.87**	**0.63**	**0.87**
	CalCom3	0.89***	16.70	0.80			
	CalCom4	0.81***	15.49	0.65			
	CalCom5	0.74***	14.29	0.55			
Online Trust	OnTr1	0.79***		0.62	**0.83**	**0.55**	**0.82**
	OnTr3	0.57***	11.71	0.33			
	OnTr4	0.75***	15.91	0.56			
	OnTr5	0.84***	17.92	0.70			

Construct	Item code	Factor Loading	t value	R² value	CR	AVE	α
Customer Loyalty	CuLo2	0.66***	Fixed	0.44	**0.86**	**0.56**	**0.85**
	CuLo3	0.73***	12.98	0.54			
	CuLo4	0.75***	13.29	0.57			
	CuLo5	0.81***	14.01	0.65			
	CuLo6	0.77***	13.46	0.59			

***p < 0.001

Convergent and Discriminant Validity

To evaluate the convergent validity of the construct measures, the factor loadings for each item was evaluated. As observed in Table 9.7, all individual items measuring each construct had high factor loadings and were each statistically significant at p < 0.001. Also, the AVE of each construct was analysed to test convergent validity. AVE values greater than 0.5 connote the validity of both the construct and the individual items (Luarn & Lin, 2005). Table 9.7 shows that the AVE of each construct is greater than 0.5, thereby indicating convergent validity. To evaluate discriminant validity, the AVEs and the shared variance between the construct were compared. According to Lu, Zhou, Bruton & Li (2010) the condition to satisfy discriminant validity is that the AVE for each construct must be greater than the corresponding inter-construct square correlation. The result of this analysis is presented in Table 9.8.

TABLE 9.8 CORRELATION MATRIX WITH AVEs

Construct	Standard Deviation	Mean	1	2	3	4	5
1 - Interactivity	1.16	3.49	(0.79)				
2 - Engagement	1.20	2.60	0.49	(0.76)			
3 - Calculative Commitment	0.92	3.49	0.04	0.04	(0.87)		
4 - Online Trust	0.71	4.08	0.53	0.28	0.10	(0.83)	
5 - Customer Loyalty	0.65	3.98	0.08	0.09	0.44	0.32	(0.86)

Diagonal elements are the AVEs; Off-diagonal elements are the squared correlations

From the table, it can be gathered that the AVEs are consistently greater than the squared correlations obtained between the constructs. Therefore, it can be concluded that the constructs measured satisfy the conditions for discriminant validity (see Table 9.8).

Stage 2 - Structural Model

Once the measurement model had been proven to be reliable and validated with a satisfactory fit, a structural model was then tested and presented. Amos 22 was once again utilised to analyse the hypothesised structural relationships between the constructs. Prior to performing the analysis single indicants were created for each of the latent variables, in order to reduce model complexity (Boso, Oghazi & Hultman, 2017).

A diagrammatic representation of the results of the structural modelling of the hypothesised paths is given in Figure 9.3. The results of the hypotheses tests are summarised in Table 9.9. Figure 9.3 shows the standardized path coefficients, their significance levels and R^2 values, which indicate the amount of variance explained by the independent variables. The values of the fit statistics for the structural model were all found to be well within the acceptable limits: χ^2 (Chi-square) = 13.3, df (degrees of freedom) = 6 and χ^2/df ratio = 2.2. Comparative Fit Index (CFI) = 0.99, Incremental Fit Index (IFI) = 0.99 and Tucker-Lewis Index (TLI) = 0.96; Root Mean Square Error of Approximation (RMSEA) = 0.05 and Standardised Root Mean Square Residual (SRMR) = 0.03.

FIGURE 9.3 HYPOTHESIZED STRUCTURAL MODEL

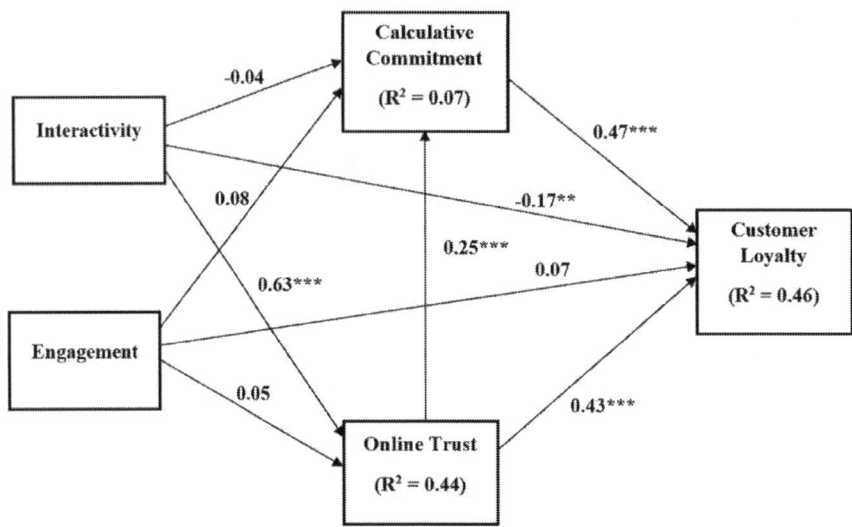

χ^2 (Chi-square) = 13.3, df (degrees of freedom) = 6, p = 0.04, χ^2/df = 2.2, RMSEA = 0.05. **p < 0.01, ***p < 0.001

TABLE 9.9 HYPOTHESES TEST RESULTS

Hypothesised Path	Standardized Coefficients	t value	p value	Results
H_1 Engagement → Calculative Commitment	0.08	1.22	0.22	Not supported
H_2 Interactivity → Calculative Commitment	-0.04	-0.52	0.60	Not supported
H_3 Engagement → Customer Loyalty	0.07	1.46	0.14	Not supported
H_4 Interactivity → Customer Loyalty	-0.17	-2.98	**	**Supported**
H_5 Engagement → Online Trust	0.05	1.05	0.29	Not supported
H_6 Interactivity → Online Trust	0.63	12.61	***	**Supported**
H_7 Online Trust → Calculative Commitment	0.25	4.07	***	**Supported**

Hypothesised Path	Standardized Coefficients	t value	p value	Results
H₈ Calculative Commitment → Customer Loyalty	0.47	12.67	***	Supported
H₉ Online Trust → Customer Loyalty	0.43	8.94	***	Supported

**p < 0.01, ***p < 0.001

Hypothesis 1 predicted that engagement has a positive impact on calculative commitment. There was no statistical support for this path (t = 1.22, p = 0.22); therefore Hypothesis 1 is not supported. Similarly, Hypothesis 2 posited that interactivity has a positive influence on calculative commitment and Hypothesis 3 posited that engagement has a positive influence on customer loyalty. However, there was a lack of support for both hypotheses; resulting in an insignificant result for Hypothesis 2 (t = -0.52, p = 0.60) and Hypothesis 3 (t = 1.46, p = 0.14). Furthermore, the findings provided support for Hypothesis 4 (t = -2.98, p < 0.01), which predicted that interactivity has a significant positive influence on customer loyalty. Yet, the findings failed to find support for Hypotheses 5 (t = 1.05, p = 0.29), which predicted that engagement has a significant effect on online trust.

Nonetheless, Hypotheses 6, 7, 8 and 9 were all supported, such that interactivity was found to have a positive significant influence on online trust (t = 12.61, p < .001) and online trust was found to have a positive significant influence on calculative commitment (t = 4.07, p < .001). While calculative commitment had a significant positive impact on customer loyalty (t = 12.67, p < .001) and online trust had a significant positive impact on customer loyalty (t = 8.94, p < .001). Overall, Hypotheses 4, 6, 7, 8 and 9 were proven. Whereas, Hypotheses 1, 2, 3 and 5 were rejected.

In respect of the control variables, the study found that age (t = 0.09, p = 0.01) is positively related to customer loyalty. Therefore, a chi-square difference test was conducted to determine whether there were significant differences among the various age groups regarding the model. However, the findings revealed that there were no significant differences among the age groups (χ^2 (Chi-square) = -11.501, df = 44, p = 1.0). Nevertheless, gender (t = -0.03, p = 0.45) and the respondent's familiarity with the bank's online activities (t = -0.04, p = 0.24) had no significant impact on the customer loyalty in the model. The structural model was estimated as a baseline model with partial mediation, having all the hypothesised paths represented. However, a few of the hypothesised paths, namely Hypotheses 1, 2, 3 and 5 were rejected. Thus, to exclude the possibility of alternative explanations, a series of alternative models were tested and compared against the baseline model.

Model Comparison

The approach of testing and comparing alternative models against a baseline model, as proffered by Anderson and Gerbing (1988) involves testing a series of nested models against a baseline model by eliminating non-significant paths sequentially, in order to obtain a more parsimonious final model (Lu *et al.*, 2010).

The paths of the four unsupported hypotheses were consecutively constrained to zero one at a time in Models 1, 2, 3 and 4, after which a full mediation model was tested in Model 5; where all the direct paths from the ORM activities to the outcome variables were constrained leaving only the indirect paths. The results of this model comparison test are presented in Table 9.10. A significant change observed in the chi-square difference between the baseline model and the test model, suggested that the path constrained to zero was important and therefore provided support for the baseline model.

TABLE 9.10 RESULTS OF ALTERNATIVE MODEL COMPARISONS

Model	χ^2	df	$\Delta\chi^2$	Δdf	χ^2/df	CFI	RMSEA	SRMR
Baseline model	13.3	6	-	-	2.2	0.99	0.05	0.03
Model 1	14.8	7	$\Delta\chi^2$ (b, m1) = 1.5*	1	2.1	0.99	0.05	0.03
Model 2	13.6	7	$\Delta\chi^2$ (b, m2) = 0.3	1	1.9	0.99	0.05	0.03
Model 3	15.4	7	$\Delta\chi^2$ (b, m3) = 2.1*	1	2.2	0.99	0.05	0.03
Model 4	14.4	7	$\Delta\chi^2$ (b, m4) = 1.1*	1	2.1	0.99	0.05	0.03
Model 5	22.2	8	$\Delta\chi^2$ (b, m5) = 8.9**	2	2.8	0.98	0.05	0.03

*p < 0.05, **p < 0.01

Baseline model: partial mediation (with direct paths from Interactivity and Engagement to Customer Loyalty)
Model 1: the path of Hypothesis 1 (Engagement → Calculative Commitment) was constrained to zero
Model 2: the path of Hypothesis 2 (Interactivity → Calculative Commitment) was constrained to zero
Model 3: the path of Hypothesis 3 (Engagement → Customer Loyalty) was constrained to zero
Model 4: the path of Hypothesis 5 (Engagement → Online Trust) was constrained to zero
Model 5: the paths of Hypotheses 3 and 4 were constrained to zero, resulting in a full mediation model

The chi-square difference tests as shown in Table 9.10 suggest that the constraint of the path of Hypothesis 2 (Interactivity → Calculative Commitment) to zero (Model 1) actually produced a model with a better set of fit indices (χ^2 = 13.6, df = 7, χ^2/ df = 1.9, p = 0.06), than the partial mediation baseline model in which the path between Interactivity and Calculative Commitment was unconstrained. This is because there was a significant improvement in the χ^2/df and the chi-square became insignificant at p = 0.06, which is the ideal scenario indicating that the model is a good fit with the observed data (Rodríguez, Plax & Kearne, 1996). Therefore, it suggests that although interactivity and calculative commitment all contribute significantly to customer loyalty, the relationship between interactivity and calculative commitment plays a trivial role in enhancing customer loyalty. Thus, the path from interactivity to calculative commitment was removed resulting in the final structural model, as presented in Figure 9.4.

FIGURE 9.4 FINAL STRUCTURAL MODEL

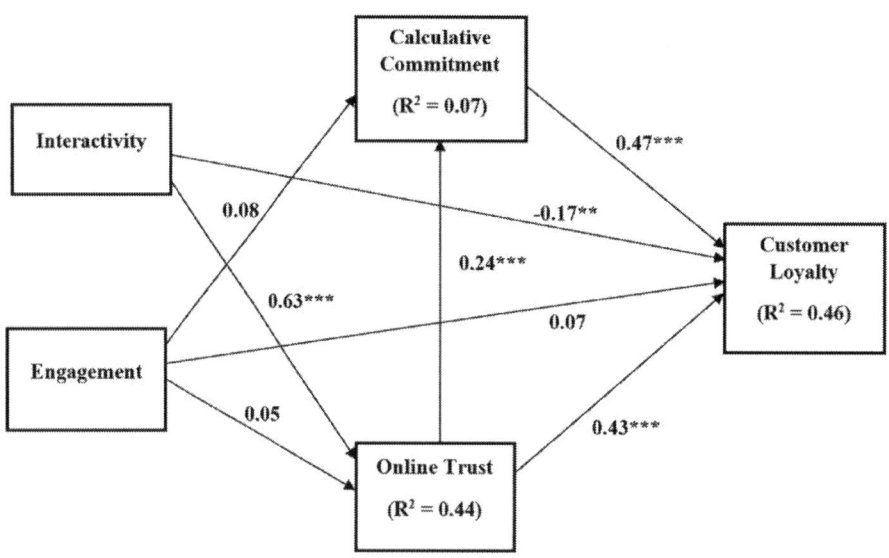

χ^2 (Chi-square) = 13.6, *df* (degrees of freedom) = 7, p = 0.06, χ^2/ *df* = 2.2, RMSEA = 0.05. **p < 0.01, ***p < 0.001

Chapter Summary

This chapter presented the analysis and results of data obtained from a sample of 429 respondents, to test the proposed hypotheses in the research model. Initially the data was screened and prepared for further analysis. The sample characteristics and the descriptive statistics were then presented, followed by an Exploratory Factor Analysis (EFA) and preliminary reliability tests. Based on the findings of the EFA, a revised research model emerged; which was then utilised in performing a Confirmatory Factor Analysis (CFA) leading to the specification of a measurement model. Subsequently, convergent and discriminant validity was assessed, showing that all the resulting measurement items were suitable and valid for additional analysis. Next, the results of the hypotheses tests obtained through the specification of the structural model were presented.

In respect of the direct relationships between the ORM activities (engagement and interactivity), the mediators (calculative commitment and online trust) and customer loyalty, Hypotheses 4, 6, 7, 8 and 9 were proven; while Hypotheses 1, 2, 3 and 5 were rejected.

REFERENCES

Academic Articles

1. Shin, Y., & Lu, Y. (2017). *Hypothesis Formulation*. Retrieved 10/10/2018 from http://methods.sagepub.com/reference/the-sage-encyclopedia-of-communication-research-methods/i6391.xml
2. Tankonyvtar (2011). Chapter 8 - Quantitative Methods Retrieved 10/10/2018 from https://www.tankonyvtar.hu/hu/tartalom/tamop412A/2011-0021_22_research_methodology/CMRM6103_Research_methodology_08.pdf.

Internet Sources

3. https://study.com/academy/lesson/what-is-a-null-hypothesis-definition-examples.html
4. http://www.statisticssolutions.com/null-hypothesis-and-alternative-hypothesis/
5. https://www.thoughtco.com/how-to-conduct-a-hypothesis-test-3126347
6. https://www.thoughtco.com/significance-level-in-hypothesis-testing-1147177

Journal Articles and Books

7. Valdez, A.D.F., Cervantes, A.V., & Motyka, S. (2018). Beauty is truth: The effects of inflated product claims and website interactivity on evaluations of retailers' websites. *Journal of the Business Research, 90*(1), 67-74.
8. Saunders, M., Lewis, P., & Thornhill, A (2009). *Research Methods for Business Students* (5th ed.). Essex, UK: Pearson Education.
9. Shaughnessy, J. J., Zechmeister, E. B., & Zechmeister, J. S. (2012). *Research Methods in Psychology* (9th ed.). New York, NY: McGraw Hill.

Internet Sources

10. https://www.simplypsychology.org/questionnaires.html
11. http://www.fao.org/docrep/w3241e/w3241e05.htm
12. http://korbedpsych.com/R09aAdopt.html

Book – Published Thesis

13. Boateng, S. L. (2018). *Online Relationship Marketing, What Works in Ghana*. Charleston, USA: Kindle Direct Publishing (an Amazon Company). ISBN-13: 978-1727453652: Available on Amazon: https://amzn.to/2QPBBMi

Internet Sources

14. http://www.rcu.co.uk/latest-news/the-10-step-guide-to-questionnaire-design/
15. http://www.marketresearchworld.net/content/view/883/
16. http://korbedpsych.com/R09bQuestionnaire.html
17. https://www.simplypsychology.org/questionnaires.html
18. https://www.fieldboom.com/likert-scale
19. http://www.statisticssolutions.com/sample-size-calculation-and-sample-size-justification/sampling/

20. https://socialresearchmethods.net/kb/sampnon.php
21. https://www.khanacademy.org/math/statistics-probability/designing-studies/sampling-methods-stats/a/sampling-methods-review
22. http://dissertation.laerd.com/probability-sampling.php
23. http://www.statisticshowto.com/probability-and-statistics/find-sample-size/

Journal Articles and Books

24. Bartlett, J. E., Kotrlik, J. W., & Higgins, C. C. (2001). Organisational research: determining organisational research: determining appropriate sample size in survey research. *Information Technology, Learning, and Performance Journal*, *19*(1), 43-50.
25. Cochran, W. G. (1977). *Sampling Techniques* (3rd ed.). New York, NY: John Wiley & Sons.
26. Yamane, T. (1967). *Statistics, An Introductory Analysis* (2nd ed.). New York, NY: Harper and Row.

Internet Sources

27. https://www.socialresearchmethods.net/kb/statdesc.htm
28. https://www.dummies.com/education/math/statistics/how-to-interpret-standard-deviation-in-a-statistical-data-set/
29. https://statistics.laerd.com/spss-tutorials/principal-components-analysis-pca-using-spss-statistics.php
30. http://psych.wisc.edu/henriques/mediator.html

Journal Articles and Books

31. Boateng, S. L., & Narteh, B. (2016). Online Relationship Marketing and affective customer commitment – The mediating role of trust. *Journal of Financial Services Marketing*, *21*(2), 127-140.

Internet Source

32. http://statwiki.kolobkreations.com/index.php?title=Structural_Equation_Modeling#Mediation

Book

33. Hair, J., Anderson, R., Tatham, R., & Black, W. (1998). *Multivariate data analysis* (5th ed.). Upper Saddle River, NJ: Prentice-Hall.

Internet Source

34. https://processpolicy.com/exploratory-factor-analysis.htm

Book

35. Tabachnick, B. G., & Fidell, L. S. (2001). *Using Multivariate Statistics* (4th ed.). New York, NY: Allyn and Bacon.

Internet Source

36. http://www.statisticssolutions.com/factor-analysis-sem-exploratory-factor-analysis/

Journal Articles and Books

37. Hair, J. F., Black, W. C., Babin, B. J., & Anderson, R. E. (2010). *Multivariate Data Analysis* (7th ed.). Upper Saddle River, NJ: Prentice Hall.

38. Comrey, A. L. (1973). *A first course in factor analysis*. New York, NY: Academic Press.
39. Kaiser H. F. (1970). A second-generation little jiffy. *Psychometrika, 35*(4), 401-415.
40. Bartlett M. S. (1950). Tests of significance in factor analysis. *British Journal of Psychology, 13*(Part II), 77-85.
41. Henson R. K., & Roberts J. K. (2006). Use of exploratory factor analysis in published research: Common errors and some comment on improved practice. *Educational and Psychological Measurement, 66*(3), 393-416.
42. Kuhl, E. A., Dixit, N. K., Walker, R. L., Conti, J. B., & Sears, S. F. (2006). Measurement of patient fears about implantable cardioverter defibrillator shock: An initial evaluation of the Florida Shock Anxiety Scale. *Pacing and Clinical Electrophysiology, 29*(6), 614-618.
43. Costello, A. B., & Osborne, J. W. (2005). Best practices in exploratory factor analysis: Four recommendations for getting the most from your analysis. *Practical Assessment, Research & Evaluation, 10*(7), 1-9.
44. Zikmund W. G., Babin B. J., Carr J. C., & Griffin M. (2009). *Business Research Methods* (8th ed.). Mason, OH: South-Western College Publishing.
45. Krabbe, P. F. M. (2017). *The Measurement of Health and Health Status. Concepts, Methods and Applications from a Multidisciplinary Perspective* (1st ed.). London, UK: Academic Press.
46. Pallant, J. (2011). *SPSS Survival Manual: A Step by Step Guide to Data Analysis Using SPSS for Windows* (4th ed.). Berkshire, UK: McGraw Hill, Open University Press.
47. Christmann, A., & van Aelst, S. (2006). Robust estimation of Cronbach's alpha. *Journal of Multivariate Analysis, 97*(7), 1660-1674.
48. Kottner, J., & Streiner, D. L. (2010). Internal consistency and Cronbach's α: A comment on Beeckman et al. (2010). *International Journal of Nursing Studies, 47*(7), 926-928.
49. Botha, E., & Van der Waldt, D.L.R. (2011). Relationship outcomes as measurement criteria to assist communication strategists to manage organisational relationships. *Revista Innovar Journal, 21*(40), 5-16.
50. Neuman, W. L. (2014). *Social Research Methods: Qualitative and Quantitative Approaches* (7th ed.). Pearson New International Edition. Essex, UK: Pearson Education Limited.

Internet Source

51. https://courses.lumenlearning.com/suny-hccc-research-methods/chapter/chapter-7-scale-reliability-and-validity/

Journal Articles and Book

52. Bagozzi, R. P., & Yi, Y. (2012). Specification, Evaluation, and Interpretation of Structural Equation Models. *Journal of the Academy of Marketing Science, 40*(1), 8-34.
53. Kline, R. B. (2011). *Principles and Practice of Structural Equation Modelling* (3rd ed.). New York, NY: Guilford Press.
54. Fornell, C., & Larcker, D. F. (1981). Evaluating structural equation models with unobservable variables and measurement error. *Journal of Marketing Research, 18*(1), 39-50.

Internet Source

55. http://userwww.sfsu.edu/efc/classes/biol710/path/SEMwebpage.htm

Journal Article

56. Tarka, P. (2018). An overview of structural equation modelling: Its beginnings, historical development, usefulness and controversies in the social sciences. *Quality & Quantity, 52*(1), 313-354.

Internet Source

57. https://wolfweb.unr.edu/~zal/STAT755/appendix-sems.pdf

Journal Article and Book

58. Park, H., & Kim, Y. K. (2014). The role of social network websites in the consumer-brand relationship. *Journal of Retailing and Consumer Services, 21*(4), 460-467.
59. Schumacker & Lomax (2010) A beginner's guide to Structural Equation Modelling (3rd ed.). New York, NY: Taylor and Francis Group, LLC.

Internet Source

60. http://www2.gsu.edu/~mkteer/identifi.html

Journal Articles and Book

61. Iacobucci, D. (2010). Structural equations modelling: fit Indices, sample size, and advanced topics. *Journal of Consumer Psychology, 20*(1), 90-98.
62. Schreiber, J. B. (2008). Core reporting practices in structural equation modelling. *Research in Social and Administrative Pharmacy, 4*(2), 83-97.
63. Lombardi, L., & Pastore, M. (2012). Sensitivity of fit indices to fake perturbation of ordinal data: a sample by replacement approach. *Multivariate Behavioural Research, 47*(4), 519-546.
64. Byrne, B. M. (2010). *Structural Equation Modelling with Amos: Basic Concepts, Applications, and Programming* (2nd ed.). New York, NY: Taylor and Francis Group.
65. Anderson, J. C., & Gerbing, D. C. (1988). Structural equation modelling in practice: a review and recommended two-step approach. *Psychological Bulletin, 103*(3), 411-423.
66. Barreda, A. A., Bilgihan, A., Nusair, K., & Okumus, F. (2015). Generating brand awareness in online social networks, *Computers in Human Behaviour, 50,* 600-609.

INDEX

Categorical And Continuous Variables, 16
Cluster Sampling, 56
Common Method Variance, 190
Confirmatory Factor Analysis, 150, 167
Convenience Sampling, 57
Convergent Validity, 133
Dependent, Independent And Control Variables, 18
Descriptive Statistics, 66
Descriptive Statistics, 183
Discriminant Validity, 133
Exploratory Factor Analysis, 82, 89
Exploratory Factor Analysis, 186
Hypotheses, 22
Hypothesis Testing, 25
Hypothesizing Relationships Between Variables, 23
Mediating And Moderating Variables, 19
Model Comparison, 204
Non-Probability Or Non-Random Sampling, 56
Path Analysis, 152, 173
Preliminary Data Preparation, 180
Purposive Sampling, 56
Quantitative Research, 12
Questionnaire Design, 33
Questionnaire Layout, 42
Quota Sampling, 57
Reliability and Validity, 116
Sampling
   Determining Appropriate Sample Size, 58
   Selecting a Sample, 54
Selecting a Quantitative Data Analysis Technique, 14
Simple Random Sampling, 55
Snowball Sampling, 58
Stratified Random Sampling, 55
Structural Equation Modelling, 149
   Explained, 138
   Performing SEM Analysis, 141
   SEM Nomenclature, 139
   SEM Notation, 140
   Two-StageModelling, 150
STRUCTURAL EQUATION MODELLING, 191
Systematic Sampling, 55

Author Profile

Dr. Sheena Lovia Boateng is a marketing consultant and the Executive Director for the PearlRichards Foundation. She is a member of the Editorial Advisory Board of the *Emerging Markets Case Studies*, published by Emerald Publishing. She holds Doctoral and Undergraduate degrees in Marketing from the University of Ghana. She is the first female to complete a PhD in Marketing from the University of Ghana and is also the founder of the Women in Tertiary Education (WITE) Network, which seeks to provide support for women in tertiary education concerning academic research, family-life and career balance.

During her undergraduate program, Dr. Boateng was one of three students chosen to pursue an E-commerce and International Marketing program at the Harstad University College, Norway. She was selected out of a class of 235 students. In Norway her group research project on the "Influence of color on consumer purchase intention" won the University's best thesis award. In 2013, she was upgraded from her MPhil Marketing degree program to begin a PhD Marketing degree program at the University of Ghana Business School. This was after scoring grade A in all twelve courses undertaken in the first year of the MPhil program. She subsequently progressed to become the First Doctoral Student in University of Ghana to present a conference paper and a doctoral consortium paper at the Academy of Marketing Conference (2015), Limerick, Ireland.

Dr. Sheena Boateng's research interests include relationship marketing, digital marketing, fashion marketing, marketing in micro and small businesses, and electronic learning. She has expertise in enabling companies to develop products and services to respond to the dynamics of consumer behavior. Her consultancy work includes training 400 micro-enterprises across the country for Ministry of Finance and developing case studies on Ghanaian firms for the World Bank – to showcase innovative Ghanaian Manufacturing firms.

Since beginning her doctoral career, she has collaborated with other faculty from different universities to obtain not less than US $200,000 in research and project funds. These research and project funds have been obtained from organizations including Danish International Development Agency (DANIDA), World Bank and United States International Development Agency (USAID) and the African Development Bank (AFDB). She recently developed a certificate program in Fashion Marketing and Promotion and subsequently, trained the 30 fashion entrepreneurs in the program. She has published five journal publications, four published conference papers, three book chapters, one working paper and two books in marketing. Her academic work has been published in the *Journal of Financial Services Marketing, Smart Learning* and the *Journal of Educational Technology Systems* and *the International Journal of Bank Marketing.*

Printed in Great Britain
by Amazon